I0484660

Monster Filmmaking

How to make a feature film in 7 Easy Steps

Written and directed by

Ayhan Ozden

Table of contents

7 Entering the Festivals

7. 1Preparing the Teaser

7.2 Gathering All the Documents

7.3 Entering the Festivals

7.4 Interviews

7.5 Distribution is HARD or NOT?

7.6 This is Your Business Card Baby!

7.7 Cinema Club

7.8 Making Your Own DVDs and Blu-Rays

7.9 Say Goodbye to your Baby

Introduction

Ok, first take a deep breath, fasten your seat belts. This will be fast for all of us, movie lovers! We are all going to transform from a movie lover to a MOVIE MAKER!

 Like all the transition processes it may be a little bit hard at the beginning. However, as we follow the 9 Easy Steps it will get easier and easier. Like everyone of us who are interested creating something, it all starts with an idea. Whether it's a book, movie or an art piece of any kind.

 We all know that ideas are important. However without the execution there will be nothing but just a small talk between friends. In this book you are going to take a big further step to the glory of making something out of nothing. Just your idea will be enough.

 With following the 7 easy steps, you are going to make your genius idea into a great feature film.

For those of you who have already started making short films, it will be a great journey and a good challenge for you. I might know what you think right now! It seems impossible to jump from a short film to a featurette, but as you go on reading the book you are going to realize the power in you, and that you have the courage to start to a feature film.

If you are someone without any experience of a short film, do not worry; in this book you will create one, then you will find the courage. It is all about building the blocks of your new "Movie House" by easy 7 steps.

At first as you go on reading the easy 7 steps, you may find it a little bit unorthodox. But as you dig deeper you are going to understand my approach.

You already know those methods, you already have started making your own feature film without even noticing it by deciding to buy and read this book.

1.1 Start With The Basics

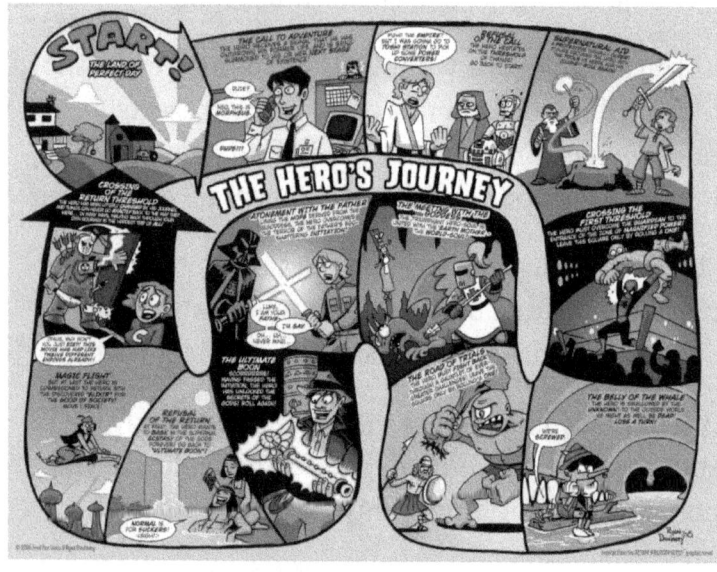

I know that everyone of us want to grasp our Dslr s and shoot the coolest videos ever. When I first started making short films, that was my only intention. I am not ashamed to say that, those times when I first begin film making I thought making a movie was all about cinematography. Getting coolest picture of the actor or the place will make me the best director ever. Also I thought that when my friends watch what I have shot, they will all understand that I am going to be a big time director! As you may already know it is not like that at all. And I had to learn that the hard way.

Of course it is important to get the right cinematography, however without telling nothing to the audience, it will be hard to be a filmmaker. You may as well get to be a good cinematographer though. If you have already shoot one or more shorts, you may as well know that a good script is the most important thing for a movie. For a good script you need a good film idea!

It is important that we should all know, there are no new stories, only versions of the old stories that you will tell in your own way. You may find this idea interesting or untrue, as I did, when I first encountered this, but it is true and a great writer Joseph Campell tells this argument in a very long and nice way in his epic, must have cinema book "The Warrior's Way". Let's not get too serious! Even though reading Joseph Campell's book may help you to understand how to write a good story, it is not rocket science. What you need is a protagonist as we may all call 'Our Hero'. Our hero's journey always begins in a place, then at the end, he returns to that place as a changed man or woman, as you will see in a detailed way in the second chapter of the book.

 Now you know that you do not need to discover America again. It is a relief for most of us, for others I know that you will try to discover it again. No problem, the limit is the sky. But never forget that what we are trying to achieve is to make a movie! So it is crucial that you don't waste too much time to find the best idea. Your ideas in your head are already the best ones. Remember you are the creator of your universe! So just pick the idea that you already have in your mind and as you feel it in your vain, we go on to the next part! It will be fun!

1.2 Brain Storming With Friends

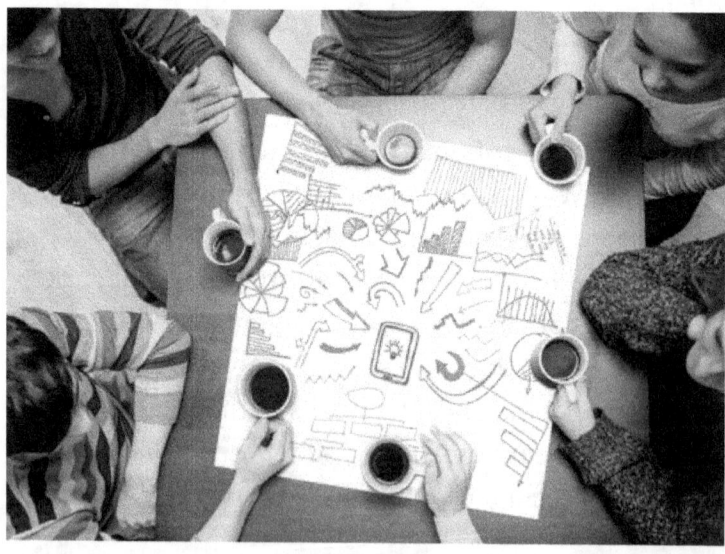

Now you have your film idea with you, it is time to share it with your friends.

This part is really important because you are making a movie not only just for your pleasure but mostly for the sake of the audience. Most of the time at the beginning, our friends and our family members will be our audience, so you might as well shape your film idea with them before starting your screenplay.

Of course it will be helpful for you to pick the right friends. What I mean by right friends, is the ones who have some interests about movies and who wouldn't judge your ideas with a bad criticism just to criticise it. If your protagonist has a specific condition or a job, you can as well start your research with your friends or relatives.

When you pick all the right friends and relatives, tell your film idea and get some feedback. You will be amazed how much you can improve your film idea with that kind of brain storming session.

1.3 Inspire From The Best

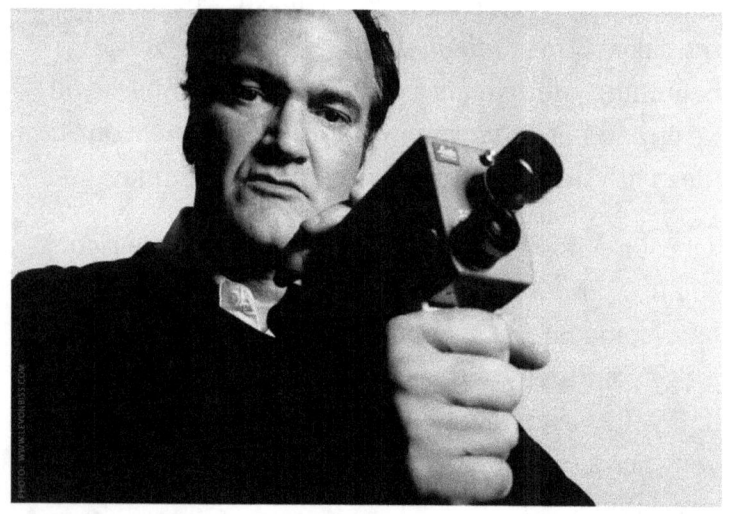

I know, it sounds cliche! However if Tarantino and most of the other big guys do it why shouldn't we? We all know the saying, right ' Great directors copy, best ones steal !'

As you already know Quentin Tarantino likes to copy Japanese movies. He also likes to watch and get inspired from the old classics and B rated movies. As you are searching for your film idea you might as well watch those kinds of movies and get inspired from them.

Actually this is not my style. I believe that every person has a different way of telling stories, and that is what makes the story/ movie sincere. However, this kind of technique may inspire your original idea. So give that a try. As you are going to the next part, you may already have some ideas crawling in your brain. You can feel it is coming. During the reading process if you have a film idea shaping in your brain, never waste it. Just writing it to your notes, will go along way.

1.4 Read, Read, Read

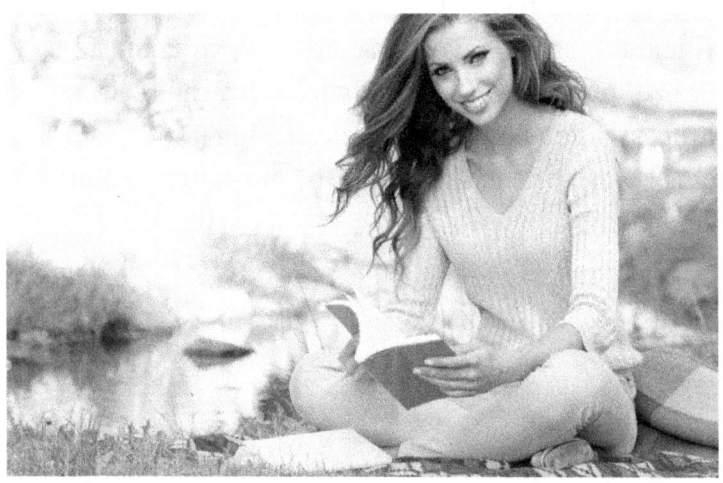

In this century it seems a little weird to read more than to watch. All the good screenplay writers and filmmakers are actually great readers.

I also have thought that I was a great reader, however it changed dramatically when I read about how much time Christopher Nolan spends on reading. His daily routine is like this; in the early morning he starts with 5 newspapers, then go on with a book for two hours. In the afternoon he reads magazines for fun. Furthermore in the evening another one hour ritual of reading a book. This is his daily routine! For his researches, he also adds lots of technical books to his daily routine.

So, why reading is that important? Because, as a filmmaker, what we do is actually, decoding words to frames. Without the 'words', we will not have something to decode. We don't have to read like Nolan. But we have to make reading a daily ritual, even if it is just for 12 minutes. You may realize, as you 'read', the film ideas will flow to you.

1.5 Analyze Your Favourite Films

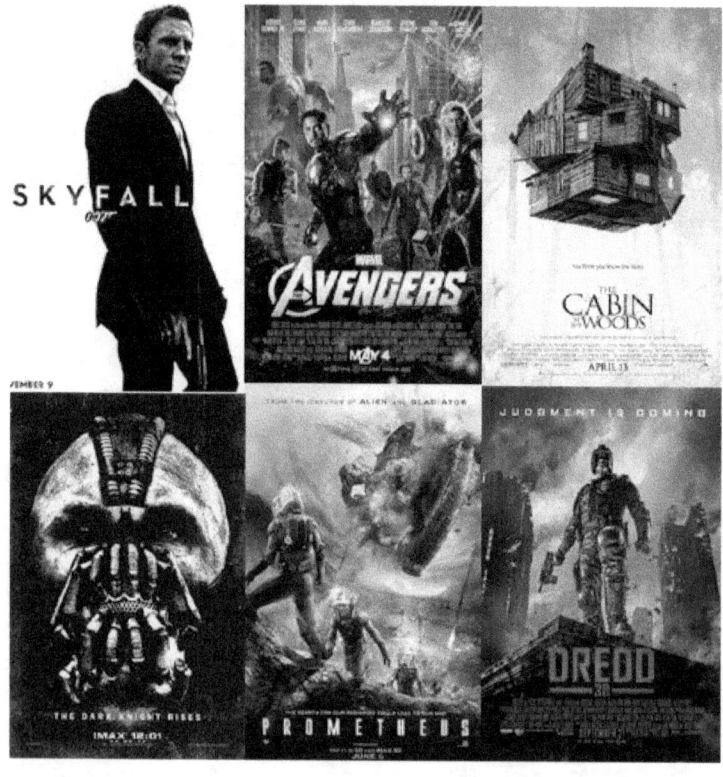

Filmmaking is a passion. We are all called 'Freaks' by most of our relatives or the people that they think they know the real us! But we know that we are just a few bunch of enthusiastic people who love movies. We all want to think of it as a way/part of our lives.

We all know that watching 5 movies back to back is just a way of our understanding about life.

Now, it is our time to watch those great movies that we've watched hundreds of times. THIS TIME VERY CAREFULLY! This time we watch them to understand why they grab our attention? What's their secret? What is their uniqueness that influence us this much? If you watch them with that perspective you will realize lots of different things about those movies. This will also inspire you to make your own unique movie.

Never forget to get notes during those watching sessions. Do not hesitate to pause the movie. Write your notes to your idea notebook. It is important to write them as one sentence. Because a good film idea is all about that 'One Good Sentence'.

1.6 Prepare Your Lucky Cards

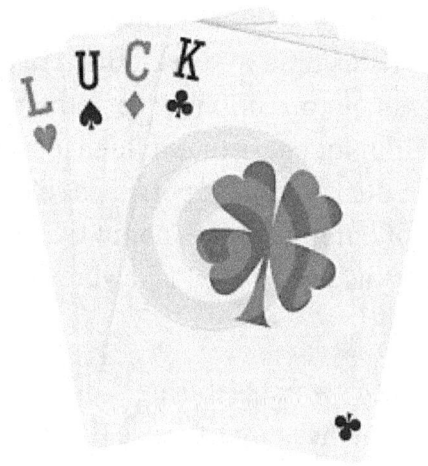

You are asking your self 'What the hack this guy is talking about right now?'. What are 'lucky cards'? Lucky Cards are the cards that you are going to write your film ideas into.

Remember your 'Idea Book' that is all the way with you during these processes. From your first film idea creation, your brain storming session with friends, analyzing your favorite movies, reading the inspirational books, you have written your ideas to that notebook. I know that you have at least 10 great ideas in your notebook, probably more.

My method deciding which of my film idea will turn into a screenplay is, to write those ideas to some small cards and pick one of them. If the first pick is not very good for you, you may have two chances left. Just go with the one. All your choices will be great, because all of them are yours.

A little hint; you can make your girl or boyfriend pick the card for you. That will make them feel really special, right?

1.7 Observe Your Self

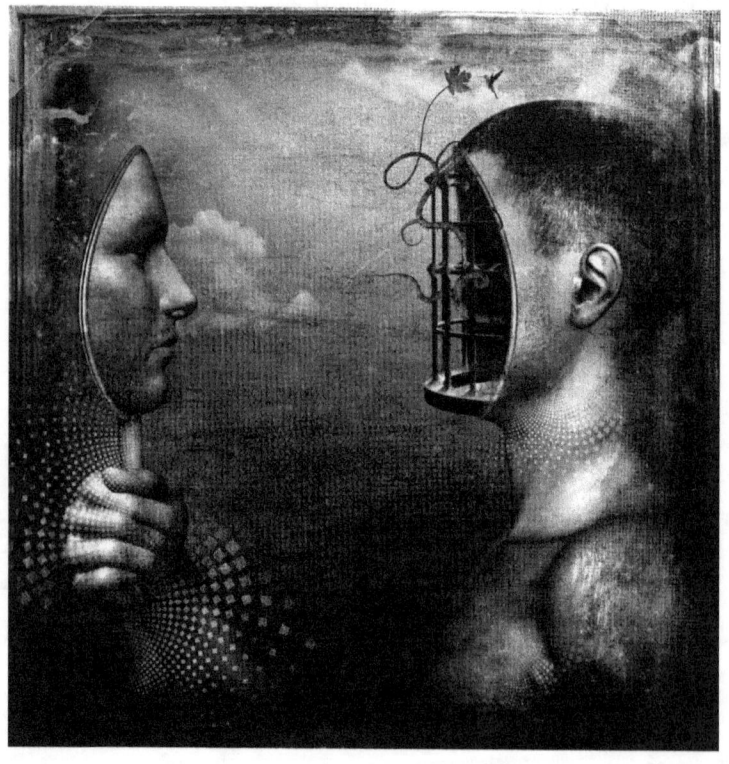

When we decide to make a movie, we are not even sure why we want to make it! Furthermore, as we start to understand the nature of filmmaking, we see that it is all about "our selves".

 Be sure about that; in filmmaking you are not telling just a story, you are telling "Your Story"! Your protagonist might be a woman, an animal, a man, a bicycle maybe; be sure that you are not telling that person or that thing, you are telling yourself.

So, you have to observe and know about yourself. You can do this, by asking yourself "Who am I?" Then ask your best friends, your family members. Always take notes to your idea book.

Remember Filmmaking is a process, which will go on for years. It is like life itself. As you make your first movie, you will know yourself better. And for your next movie you will have much more understanding about your movie style and yourself.

1.8 Simple is Always Great

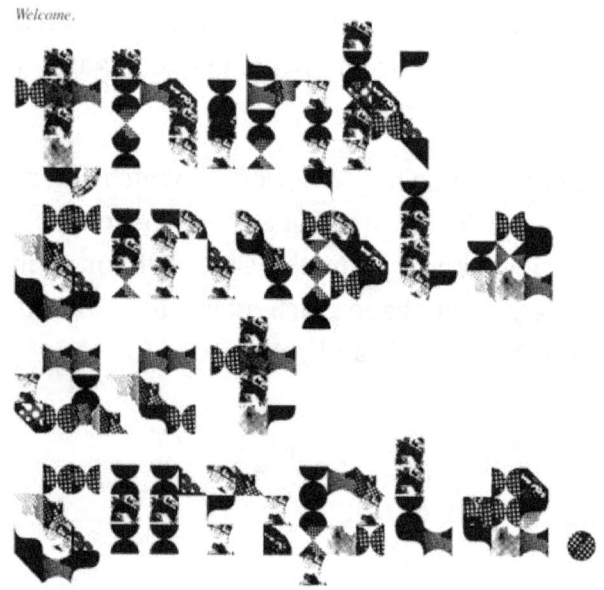

As you are reading this book, you are now realizing the power within you. In all the processes in filmmaking, we all want it to be perfect. Of course it is a good thing to plan everything and to make something perfect, however if we let this idea block us, it will slow us down. If we do slow down, we might lose our concentration during the filmmaking process.

So, at the beginning of your film career, it may be good not to be perfect, maybe just "OK"! What I mean by that is, don`t try to come with the perfect, craziest idea that will shock your audience for years. Instead of that, just pick the simplest idea that you can turn into your FIRST FEATURE FILM. This is very important, because after you finish your first feature film, your confidence will rise to the clouds. You will have a great filmmaking experience that you can show to sponsors or producers for your next movie. So don`t try too hard. Just be simple as much as you can. This will make the difference between you and the other filmmakers around.

1.9 Only One Sentence

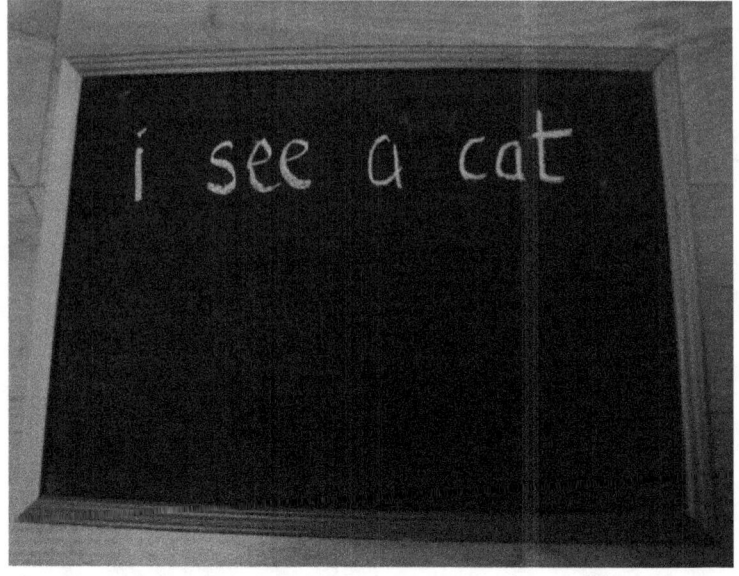

In the previous chapters you have already seen that I mentioned about this "One Sentence" thing. Why is it important to put your film idea in one sentence? Because if we can`t tell it in one sentence, then we will not be able to tell it in a movie!

When I first heard that statement during one of the best film schools in Turkey from one of my teachers, I thought that was just boloni! However time went by and when I started to pitch my film ideas to the producers, sponsors or even to the cinema professionals, they all got bored after my 5 minutes speech about my film idea. I learned it from the hard way, not to make my film ideas more than one sentence!

If you tell it in one sentence and that takes the attention, then they will be willing to hear more about your great film.

You are now ready to go to the next step. You have your one sentence film idea, which will turn into an amazing screenplay by you. Let`s move now!

As a MOVIE LOVER, we love watching movies and we don`t really grasp the idea of a good screenplay. I know that every one of us have some memorized great lines from our cult movies. Even so, screenplay writing is not just about those great lines at all!

As a Turkish filmmaker, we here have been influenced by the European cinema. You may already heard of the great director, Cannes Film Festival Awarded, Nuri Bilge Ceylan. If you have watched one of his movies, you might understand what I mean by you do not need great lines. Do not get me wrong, of course it is a great thing to have good, catchy lines in your movies, however like Nuri Bilge, most of the great directors of all times do not depend on "words"! For them filmmaking is all about "telling it without words". This may seem a little bit weird to you guys, but if you have the talent to tell your story with less words, you have what it takes to be a great director.

This may not be your style of course, but for your first feature movie, this will help your next screenplay very much.

2.1 Be Your Character

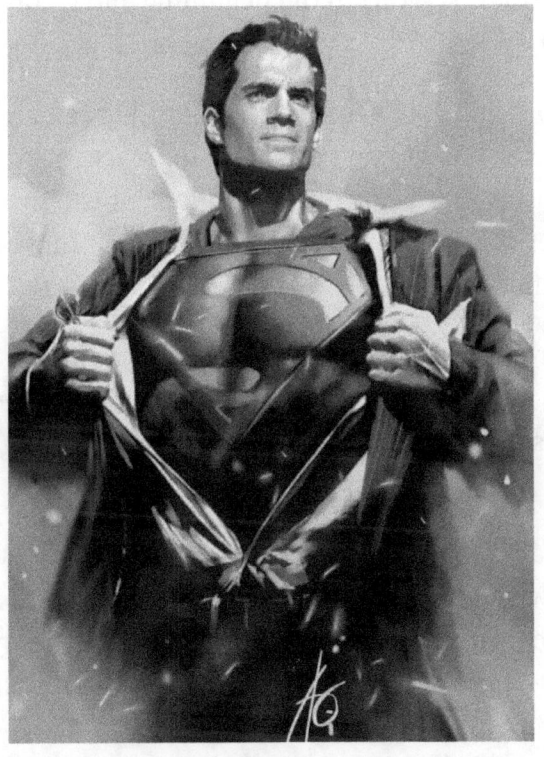

When I first started to think about writing my first screenplay, (I can still feel the horror in me) I thought that it was not possible. I didn't even know what size my font should be! (12:) What would be the character of the font?(Courier:) How many pages should I have to write for an 80 minutes feature film? (1 page = 1 minute:) Where should I write the action and separate it from the dialogues? (For the dialogues, write the character`s name in the middle of the page, do actions; start from the beginning and go on like this:)

I know this part`s title is "Be Your Character", however I want to give a brief summary for some technical details for the beginners. For the short film makers I know you already know about these boring specifics.

After learning the technical terms, I thought I was ready to write my screenplay with my great film idea. Life is not that simple, as we all know!

Before even planning your screenplay`s layout, it is crucial to know a lot about your character/s. We think that we already know them, but the ugly truth shows its face when you start writing your screenplay and don`t even know about your protagonist`s mother`s name!

As you write down your character's features you will realize that it helps you a lot to write your screenplay faster and more sincerely. Because you will have the power of your characters. You know them well. Whether it is just one sentence just write some important features of all your characters which will appear in your movie. Believe me, you will like them more as you write your screenplay. Otherwise you might be controlled by your characters. If you use CeltX software to write your screenplay, that will help you to specify your characters by asking you great questions about them.

Now you can get to the great point of this part. Be a schizophrenic, and be your character.

Now you have all your characters and your protagonists` features written. Before you start to write your screenplay, just act to your family members, to your boyfriend/girlfriend, and even in the street to strangers. I have done it for 5 days, which was really boring for my girlfriend, because my protagonist was a 7 year old mutant child:)

This method has really worked for me, because I genuinely felt him during my screenplay writing. I call this, "Method writing"! As method acting, which the great Robert DeNiro prefers, I become the guy(sometimes the girl) and never get -out of him/her during the writing process.

This may seem stupid and pointless to you, however if you do this, your protagonist will have a great insight, which in most of the film festivals the jury first looks for! Even if you do not want to participate in a film festival, or make a comedy or an action film; with this technique your character will be so real.

It is time for us to take our "real protagonist" to his
JOURNEY!

2.2 Hero`s Journey

The Hero's Journey

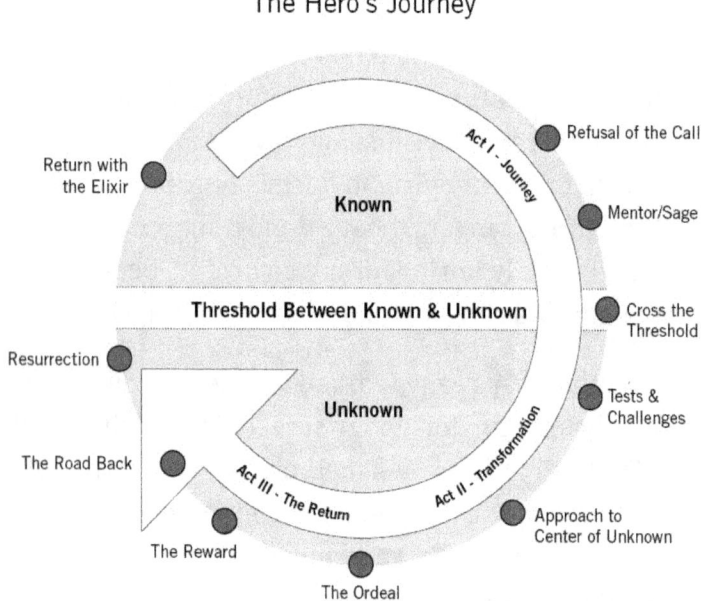

If you are new to filmmaking, you might not heard
about Hero`s Journey concept which was invented by
a great writer, Joseph Campell. I am not going to get
into the details of this of course, because there are like
100 books about it. However understanding
Campell`s concept is important for writers. Why?

Because for your film, you need a plot. Furthermore you don`t have to discover America again!

When you understand Hero`s Journey, it will be very easy to write your screenplay with great hooks in it. Your story will flow, your film will be easy to watch. Moreover, once you get it right, it will help you to create lots of variations for your next screenplays. You can find lots of great charts on the Internet, but you can check out mine too. It is really easy to follow.

When you understand Hero`s Journey just reading the key concepts from a little web search, you can combine it with my "Timeline Concept", which you are going to read in the next chapter. At the end of these easy steps, you will have so little things left to write to your screenplay.

2.3 What`s time line?

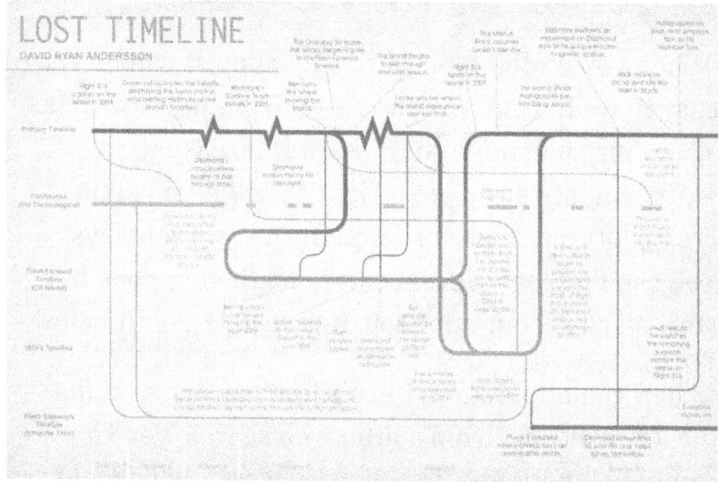

"Timeline" is a method which most of the great writers use for their screenplays`. They don`t talk about this much, but if you are a fan of great writers and follow them carefully, you may have noticed that they sometimes talk about creating a "Timeline", before they even start to write their book or screenplay. Every writer which uses this Method have different kinds of usage in their own style. I am going to talk about mine here. Of course, you can change it or make your own style of it.

I work on a big A3 size international paper, you may as well use what you want. However this size will fulfill all your needs for this workout.

Now, take the paper and draw a parallel line on it. Put 0 in the beginning, which will represent the beginning of your movie. And put 80 (or whatever minutes your film is going to be) to the end of the line which will represent the end of your movie. Put 40 in the middle, that will be the break time for it. Those points are of course the most important, this will keep you on track during the planning process.

After you finish with the key parts, it is time to mark the credits parts. Mostly for all films the beginning credits take about 4 minutes with your company logo, production companies' logo and everything. You may choose to begin with a dialogue at the beginning of the movie, even so mostly the credits parts participate with a nice music. So Mark the point in your timeline which represents the 4 minutes.

At the end credits, you may have lots of friends or companies to thank to, so the end credits will take at least 5 minutes. So mark 75 to 80 for your movie`s end credits. You see how it comes easy to structure your screenplay. After marking those parts you only have 70 pages to write. And you have the key points from the notes during the "Hero`s Journey" process. Now it is Time to put those key moments to your "Timeline". You probably have 20 key points which you have already defined before. In the timeline just write the numbers which represents those key moments for your Hero. To the down of the page you write them in front of the number. And for every key point write at least 3 sentences which define the part. You don't have to be very specific here, just write vaguely, you will be more specific later.

2.4 "10 Pages" Phenomenon

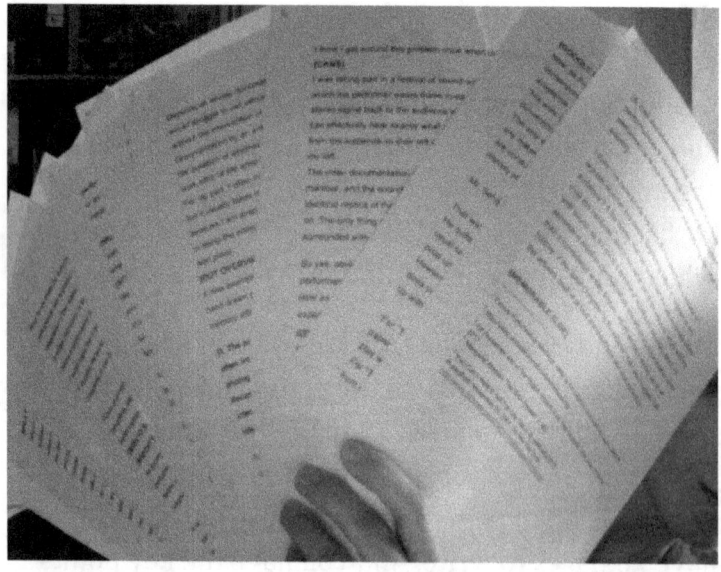

Now you have your "Timeline" in front of you. You may now visualize your movie more clearly. You have already written 20 parts in this timeline with at least 3 sentences describing the part. Why I am summarising this is; in the movie world there is a technical term called "Treatman". Treatman is a short version of your screenplay without the dialogues and details on it.

You don`t really need one if you are not pitching your film to the professionals, however it may be good for your friends who will participate and help you voluntarily for your film. Instead of reading the 80 or 90 Pages of screenplay they can easily understand the feeling of your movie by reading the 10 or 15 page treatman. This can also assist you during the screenplay writing process.

This may seem hard for others but not for you. Because as you have prepared your timeline, you already have most of your treatman. Just expand it a little, give some details. It will be a 10 pages treatman for you.

2.5 What did you dream?

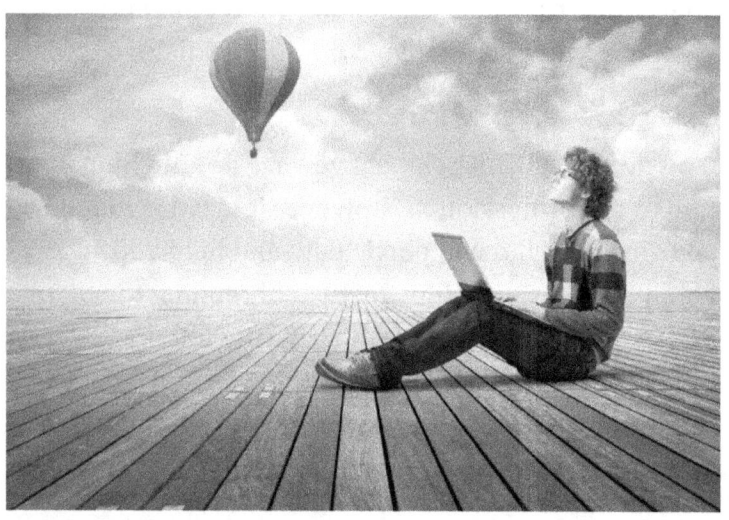

I know that we Indy filmmakers are mostly do not have big budgets or no budgets at all, and we mostly write our screenplays depending on this. Of course this blocks lots of our imagination. This shouldn't kill your creativity, instead we can use this as our power!

How? Dream as crazy as you can, dream big, bigger, bigger! You already have your character and the plot of your movie, so when you dream about this before starting your screenplay, you can expand your screenplay`s direction. If you have a friend who knows a little bit CGI, you can talk with him about your crazy dreaming and if he can implement it for your movie. By doing this you will know your limits during the writing process.

 Of course this will depend on your own budget. Maybe you are lucky enough to finance a good CGI artist for your movie, mostly we are not. But in both cases it is good to dream big and shape it a little within your budget.

2.6 Just 3 Pages A Day

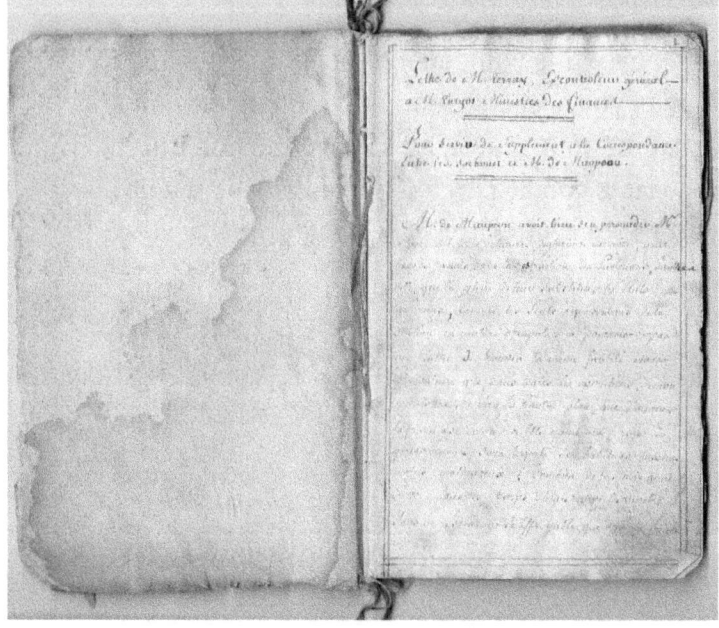

It is time for the big day. I remember the day which I started my first feature length screenplay. I ate like an elephant. Yeah that is right, I was obese. I tend to link my weight loss to my 3 Pages A Day routine. I know that there is no scientific proof behind it, however after I started this writing routine a lot has changed in my life. One of which is my weight!

Anyways, let's go on with our filmmaking! The first thing you should keep in mind is; you don't have to finish your screenplay in a day. Or a week, or a month!

It is up to you to decide. Nobody is paying you money for that, so do not worry about it.

Remember, you are half way there with your preparations before starting your screenplay. Just start writing 3 pages a day. You can separate it in two or three parts, so the only thing you have to do is to write 1 tiny page per session. It is crucial to keep your writing records in an excel sheet, so that you can put a check everyday you write.

2.7 The first draft is always "Goooood"!

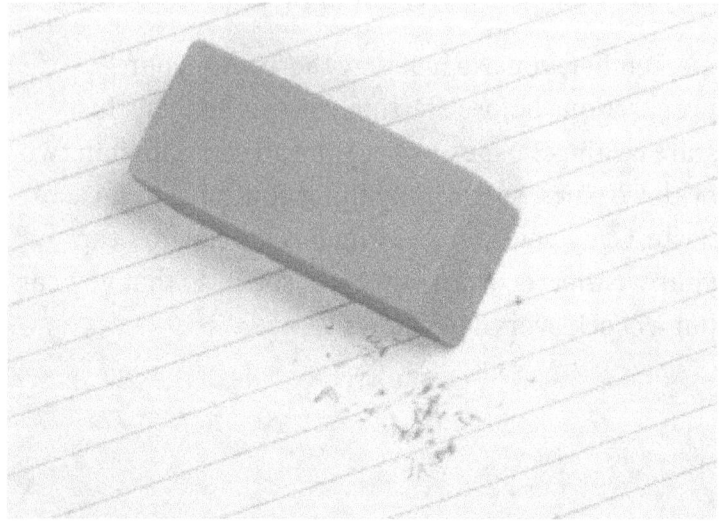

As a filmmaker, the secret for writing a good screenplay is, to understand that when you finish your screenplay it is just the first draft. More often filmmakers like us (indy filmmakers), do not give a damn about the second or the third draft of the screenplay. Because we are in a hurry to take our camera and shoot our masterpiece. However this puts a lot of pressure on most of the filmmakers. With this pressure they can not finish their screenplay! So without the screenplay, they will not have anything to shoot about!

 The first draft is just about writing down the things that you have already prepared before. You don`t have to worry about anything right now. Grammar, dialogues, etc... You can worry about those things for the second draft.

For the first draft of your screenplay you just stick to the 3 pages a day routine, and write them down. You may as well write more than 3 pages after 10 days, because you get used to the routine and want to write more. Remember, this is just the first draft, you need this for the framework so that you can work on this. As you write freely you will see that, more will come to you and it will come faster!

2.8 Don`t Want to write 2nd draft!

Now, it is time for a littlerest. As you have written the first draft of your screenplay, it will be good to take a rest and put the screenplay away for a little bit. All the great writers do this, because after finishing it, your brain needs a little rest. This is a good preparation for your second draft too.

After you are done with your resting, read your first draft with your fresh, rested brain. During the reading process take some notes if you want to change a part or a dialogue. Those notes will be your helpers for your second draft writing process. If you have a writer friend, you may share your ideas for your second draft, and reshape it with a good brainstorming session. After that, take your notes with you and start writing your second draft with your 3 pages a day routine. Never mind the grammar mistakes, you will concentrate on that in your third draft.

Just concentrate on your plot, scenes, continuity and dialogues. Do not worry; as you follow these steps it will be perfect. Furthermore, you still have your third draft to make it perfect.

2.9 The Last Action Draft

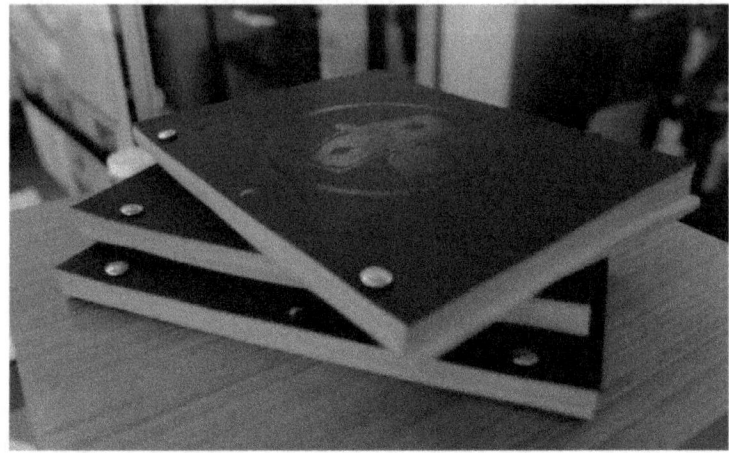

We are almost there. Your screenplay is almost ready. For the final draft, rest littlebit less than your first time out!

You can call your final draft of your screenplay, the shooting scenario. In the shooting scenario, you will give each scene a number for the shoots. This will help you for your planning for the schedule and all other things.

Also in the last draft it is time to concentrate on your grammar and the spelling. For this process, working with a friend who has a good knowledge of literature may help a lot. Also it is really hard to see your own mistakes eventough you read it five times.

After finishing your final draft, give yourself a little rest and hand your screenplay to a trustworthy friend who can be good enough to be your editor. After the editing period, your screenplay will be ready to go!

A little hint; after getting your screenplay from your editor friend, it may be a good idea to read it for the last time, before moving on to the next process.

3 Pre-production is Boring

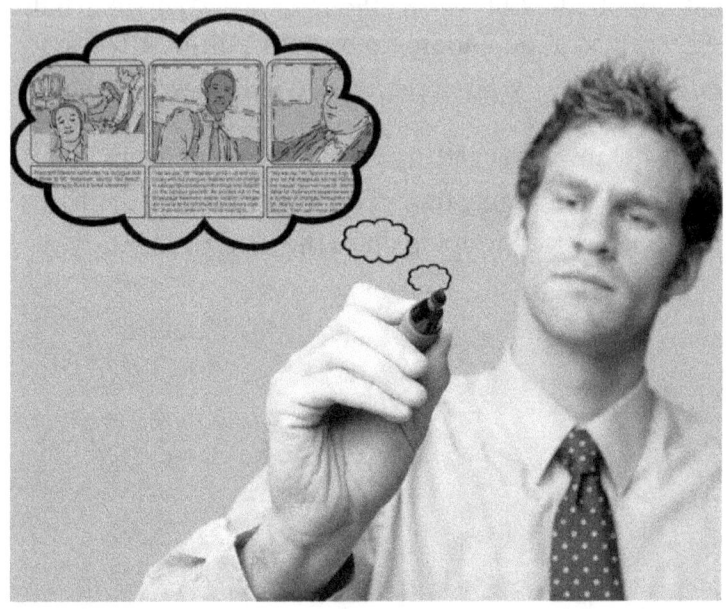

You now have your screenplay ready to shoot. If you think that it is time for you to get your camera and shoot the scenes that you have written, I am sorry but you will make your biggest mistake! Without the preparation, you will be lost in your set. You may as well be with the other amateur filmmakers and not be able to finish shooting your movie.

 However by following my methods for pre-production, you will be well prepared and can shoot your movie easily and professionally.

With your little budget or no budget I know that you are merely alone. I have been there! So what we can all do for this is, to plan carefully and think creatively. With spending little time on planning your movie, will create a great difference.

With this planning you will minimize your risk, foresee the possible barriers that may come along the way during the production process.

3.1 Scheduling the Shooting

	Monday 1-Dec	Tuesday 2-Dec	Wednesday 3-Dec	Thursday 4-Dec	Friday 5-Dec	Saturday 6-Dec	Sunday 7-Dec
1:00	Shaft	Foxy Brown	The Long Walk Home	Start the Revolution Without Me	Jefferson in Paris	Dangerous Liaisons	Smoke Signals
2:00							
3:00	Dangerous Liaisons	Smoke Signals	Start the Revolution Without Me	Dangerous Liaisons	Smoke Signals	Start the Revolution Without Me	Jefferson in Paris
4:00							
5:00	Smoke Signals	Ridicule	Dangerous Liaisons	Jefferson in Paris	Ridicule	Smoke Signals	Ridicule
6:00							
7:00	Ridicule	Dangerous Liaisons	Jefferson in Paris	Smoke Signals	Start the Revolution Without Me	Jefferson in Paris	Dangerous Liaisons
8:00							
9:00							
10:00	Jefferson in Paris	Start the Revolution Without Me	Smoke Signals	Shaft	Dangerous Liaisons	Ridicule	The Long Walk Home
11:00							
12:00							
1:00							

This is the crucial part of your pre-production process. By scheduling your shooting, you will have the ability to control the production process.

First, take a big calender in front of you. Then mark the days that you will be shooting. Of course, you will define the month which will be most suitable for you . As independent filmmakers, we mostly have the summer time for the shooting. This is also good as to weather conditions. You don`t want to shoot your scenes with your unpaid crew freezed to their souls in winter!

The second part is, to define the day and night scenes. Best times for the day scenes start at 6 a.m until 11.30 a.m which has the best light for your cinematography. You may give your crew a little rest between 12 p.m. to 1 p.m., then start shooting again. Shooting will go on till 3a.m (or maybe more) depending on your crew`s energy. In good conditions you will be able to shoot 5 pages a day which will led you to finish your shooting in two weeks depending on your shooting speed and screenplay pages.

3.2 Everybody wants Brad Pitt (Casting)

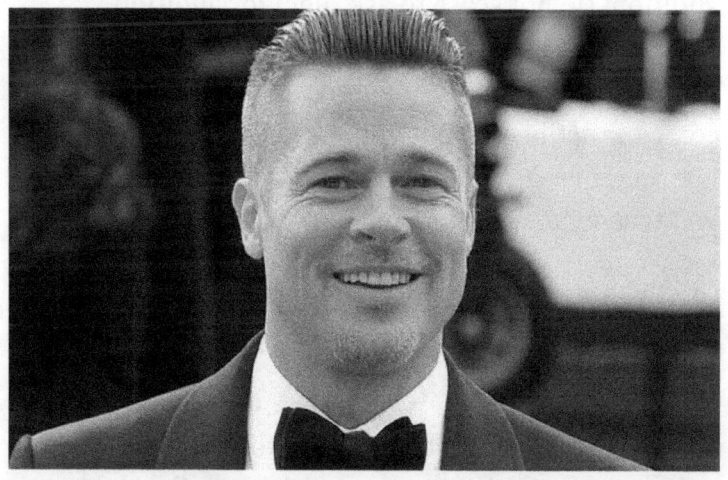

As independent filmmakers it will be hard to get Brad for our first feature movie! However never dream less! You have your screenplay now, whether it is good or bad you can always send them to some actors` agents or to some theater actors/actresses. This will create the hype for your name as a filmmaker. Although there is big chance they won`t even take a look at your screenplay, if you have time, go and meet with them and deliver your script by hand.

If this method doesn`t work out, (you never know) it is time for you to turn to your family members, relatives and friends for casting. You can choose at least two candidates for your important characters and take them in front of your camera and make an audition. Do not scare to ask them for audition because there are people who think that they can easily act like Brad or Angelina, however when it comes to acting in front of the camera they can freeze like an ice cream. Also by organizing an audition they will take you and your film more seriously.

Organizing an audition is good to look good but the important thing here is to cast the right person for your movie.

Here is the tricky part; always go for the actor/actress which is more available in the shooting period and who has the better attitude. This is a very important subject, because remember you don`t pay them for their acting and even though it seems fun at first, acting for a feature film is hard. So in the casting process always go for the one who has the motivation for that kind of challenge. You may think that acting is important for me, I will handle him/her in the movie set you may probably be wrong. Moreover making the wrong casting choice might led to cancellation of your movie during the shooting period.

After finishing with your casting always tell them about the details of your movie. Ask them nicely to memorise their lines and give them your shooting schedule.

3.3 We Need Gear Man!

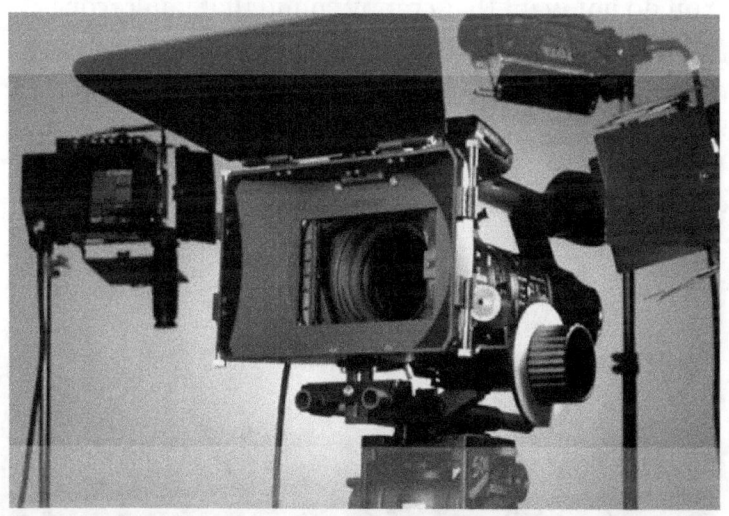

As a starter what we probably have is a Dslr. You may think that is all we need as you know about Robert Rodriguez`s El Mariachi story! However the real truth behind that story is a little bit different! (You can check the real story of it from the web, I will not go in details here)

We do not need much but if you are going for a feature film you need more than a Dslr! If you have night scenes (which you probably have) you need LIGHT! It doesn`t have to be a professional one, however with your lens set it will be hard to get your characters shine! You need at least 3 basic lights for your 3 point lighting.

Another important thing for a feature film is SOUND. You do not want that crappy sound that you record with your Dslr. What you may use is Rode boom mic, and maybe a ZoomH4N. Sometimes with Rode boom microphones you can directly connect it to your Dslr, however there will be a "hiss" problem which you need to fix in the post production process.

3.4 Places to Discover

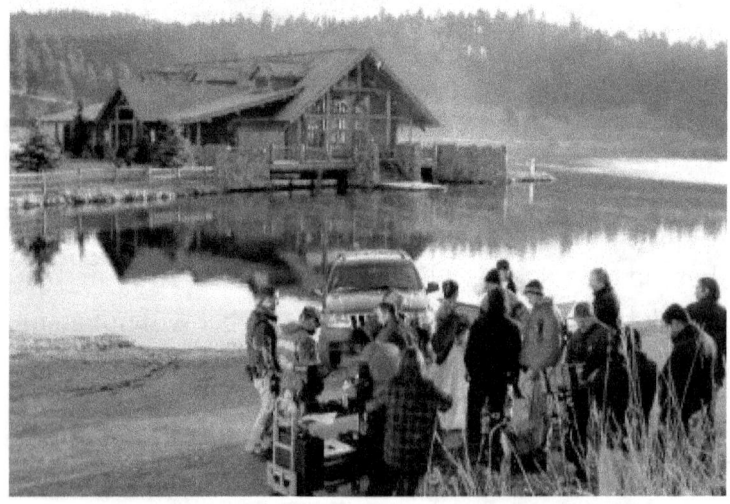

After the casting session you now need to find the places you have mentioned in your screenplay. This part is also important, because as you might not hire a professional art director, you need to figure out the places that will bring some authenticity to your movie naturally.

 In the writing process you may have already defined the places that you will shoot your scenes, however it is always good to check for authentic places. Also don`t forget to get the necessary permits if needed for your shooting. You do not want to be intercepted by the police in the middle of your shooting! However for some places, they may want some money to lend the place to you. So it is good to be prepared and not to have bad surprises !

 You might find this process unnecessary, but you will be amazed after going land scouting to see all the new and fresh ideas it will bring to you.

3.5 Asking for crew members

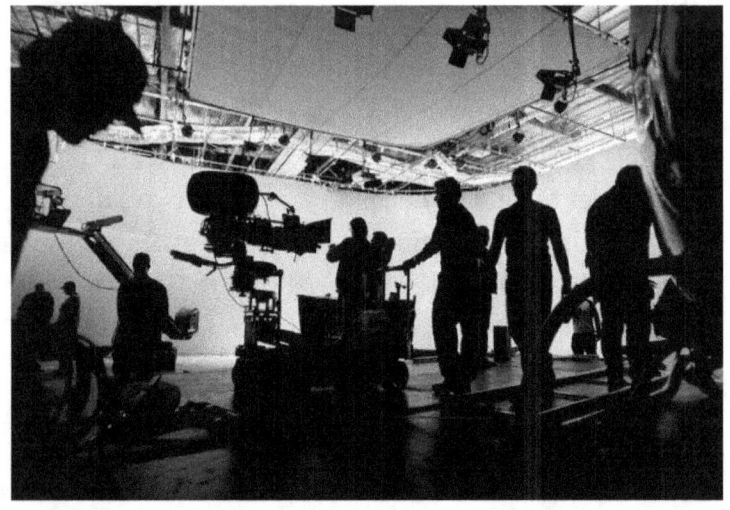

As a filmmaker you need to be outgoing. This is the nature of this life! You have to connect with people in order to understand their lives. In those meetings always search for the enthusiastic people who have the same passion like you. This will help you to get your crew members for your feature movie. You will make your own entourage by this method.

 You need a good second director, which will be your right wing, your best man who will do almost everything for you. If you are not going to do it, you need a good cinematographer or maybe a cameraman. Also you need a strong guy to hold the boom microphone for your movie to sound good.

3.6 Money is always Good!

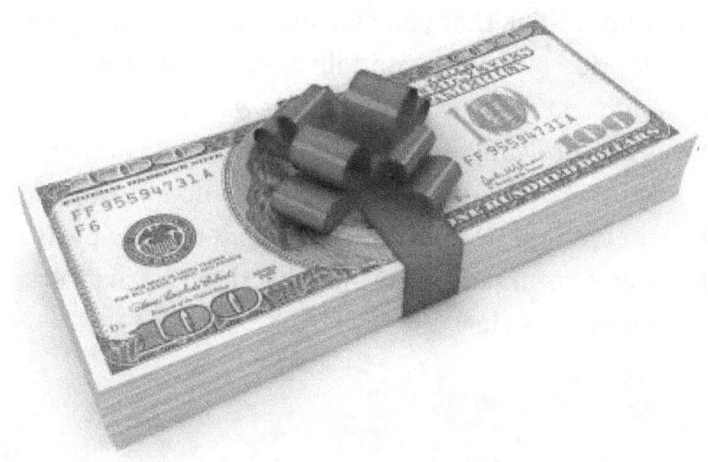

I know this sounds ridiculous to you that I`m telling indy filmmakers to find some money! However even with a good planning, not paying for your technical crew or actors you might be spending some money for your film. Some of you might already have realised this if you have shot a short film.

I am not talking about finding sponsors and making a lot of investors meeting here! No, what I am talking about is, you need to pay for the food and the gas for at least 15 days.

This might come hard to you, but you need to plan your budget before starting your shooting. With the excitement of finishing your first feature screenplay, you might think that you can just start shooting your movie! However in the middle of your shooting schedule, you may realise your crews` and actors` faces go Shrek alike! And these faces may lead them to become sick!(if you believe it, don`t) and not come to the set without even calling you about that. So please respect your unpaid crew and give them a great set environment at least.

3.7 Everybody likes to eat

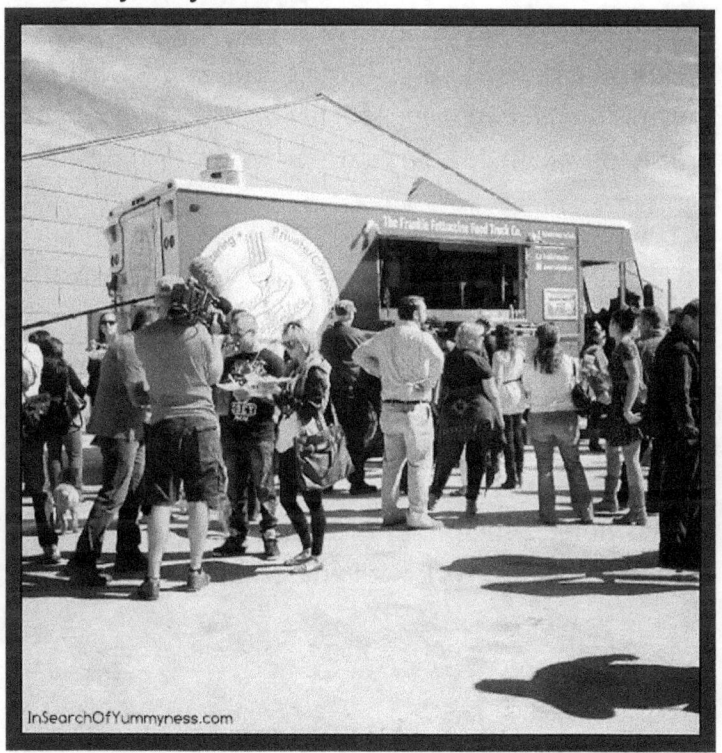

As I said in the previous part, your crew is the most important part of your movie, especially for the shooting process. So with that in mind, you can ask them what they love to eat as snacks before starting to shoot. On the first day of shooting, they will be very pleased if they see their own choices on the snacks table, be sure that you will have some great soldiers who will die with you on the set!

Your set hours will be long, so you need a lot of cafein in your set`s eating table. Also buy all kinds of crap, people like to eat crap! (Of course you know what I mean) You need to bring lots of water with you if you are shooting outside. So get them ready!

If you have enough budget you may get a catering service and make your set Hollywood like, however if you don`t have that kind of money, your mother`s mac`n cheese will be your crews` favourite. Always ask before if someone in your crew is vegetarian/vegan and ask him/her what he /she would prefer to eat. These little things will make your set harmonic which will make your movie great. And they will want to work with you again.

3.8 The Motivation Meeting

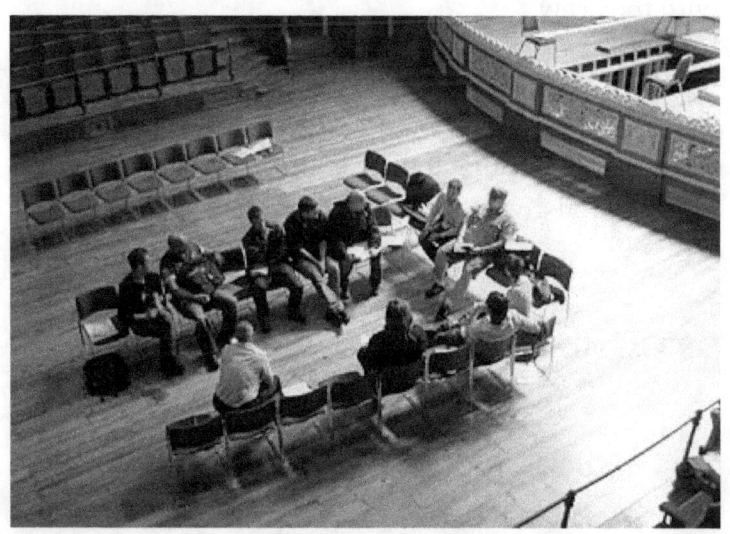

On the last days of your pre-production period, it will be good to get your crew together, so that they can get to know each other. In those meeting/s you can also read your script with your actor/actresses out loud which will also help for the shooting period.

You can organize more than one meeting if your crew's schedule is available. More meetings you have, more performance you can get from your crew.

You can inform them about their part in the production period and specify their tasks. Be clear about what they are going to be doing in the set.

Prepare your motivation speech before your meeting with the crew

 You will sound more professional like that. This is also important because everybody wants to see a director which can handle a feature film. So trust yourself and give your best motivational speech.

3.9 Visualize the Hell Out of It!

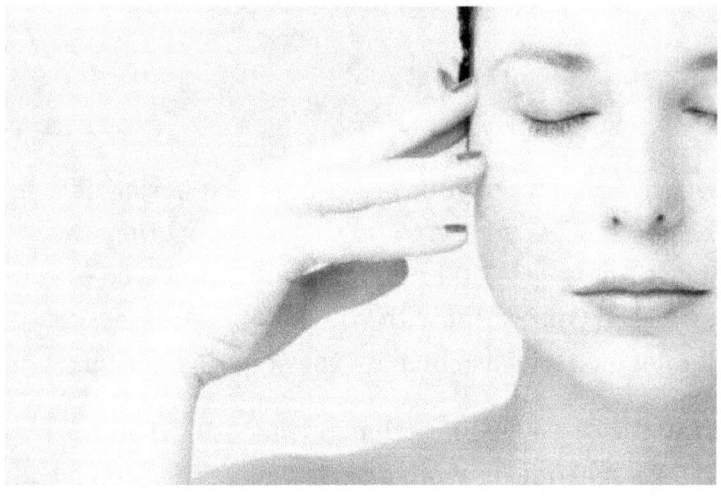

Some of you might remember the guy called Michael Jordan! One of the biggest perhaps the biggest name in the history of world basketball. I also played basketball for a long time, and I also used his method for my own game. His biggest secret was not jumping

to the sky! It was visualizing the game before playing it. There are lots of successful people who also use this method for their lives. You can use this method for your movie, especially for the shooting period.

Before the shooting day, try to visualize everything that you are going to do in the set. You can even visualize talking with your actors. This will bring more confidence to you during the shooting time which will make everything smooth.

You can use this method for every part of your movie. Remember, you are already doing this by being a filmmaker. You are making a movie that you have visualized.

4 Production

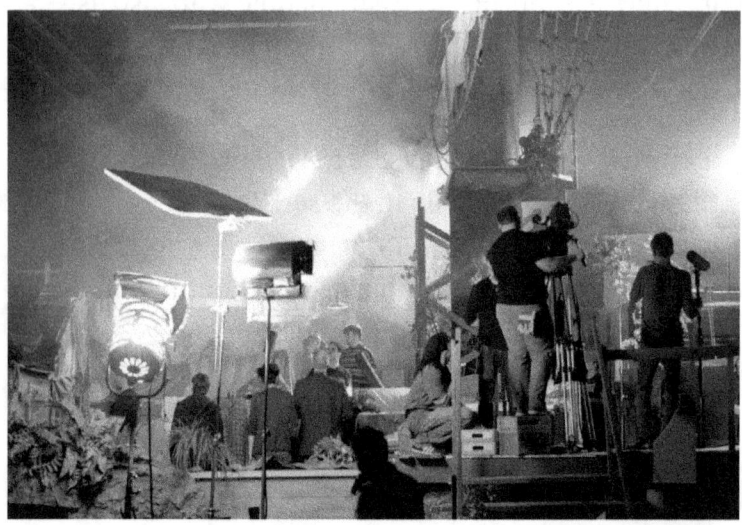

And now, it`s time for "FUN"! Finally we are there. We are going to shoot the movie that we have created in our room. We did all the preparations before and we are ready now.

You have your shooting schedule with you. It is important that you follow that schedule to finish your movie in a harmonic way. Do not worry if you are a little bit off the schedule; just put two or three days for the extra shooting. Remember you are not getting paid for your movie so don`t worry about finishing it on time. However it will be good for your crew and yourself to finish it on time so that you will be more confident for the next movie.

This process of filming comes hard for most, however if you love filmmaking this is the part which you enjoy a lot. I am not going to get in detail here, because I know that you are already ready for this. I will just give you some tips to make this process more fun and easier. So what are you waiting for? Just read the other pages and start to shoot your movie!

4.1 Who is Doing What?

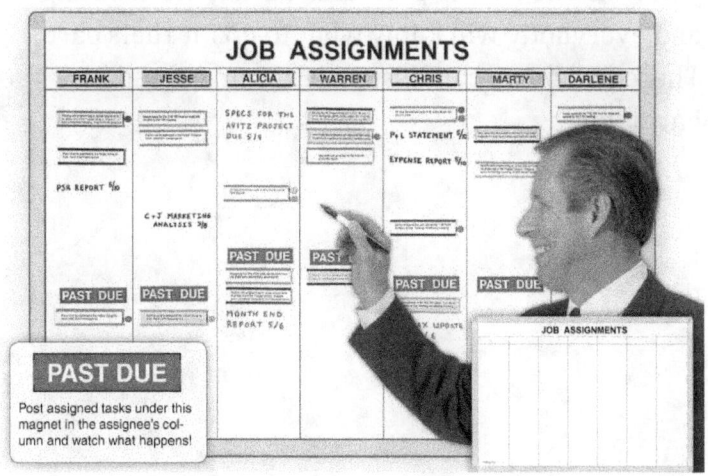

For indy filmmakers like us it can be confusing for the production period to assign jobs, because it seems like everybody is doing everything. This may be the heart of your movie but it may cause some problems. How?

First of all if you do not specify someone`s job on the set, it may be confusing for him or her to do something. Also nobody wants to do the hard stuff, what they call in a big movie set production manager. Of course in Hollywood movies` production managers, they have a lot of assistants who help them. In your set most of the time you might be responsible for the set to be ready. You sometimes have to move the chairs, set the lights and the camera by yourself. However if you assign the right person to the right job you won`t be having problems during the shooting and everybody will know what to do for their part. There will be no confussion and your set will be harmonic.

4.2 How many Pages a Day?

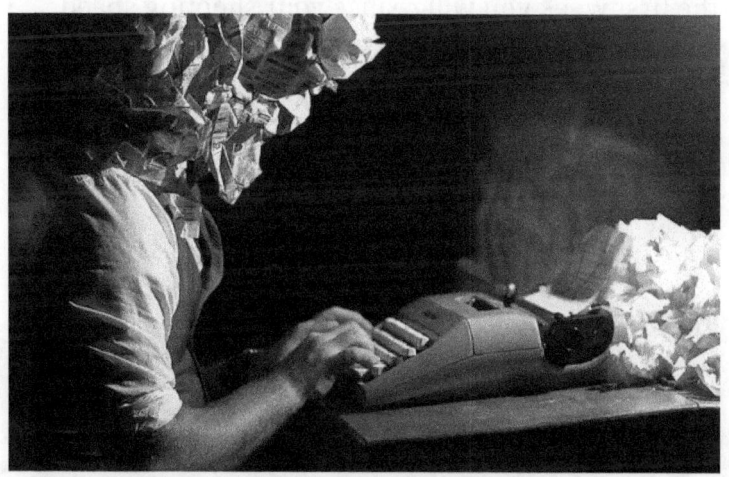

Well here is the big question! Probably you have scheduled this before in the pre–production period, however this will be your first feature film so it is a little bit different from shooting a short. Mostly it depends on your scenes but you have to follow a pattern to finish your movie.

 Ok I know that you don`t have to worry about time, but if you shoot your movie too slow it will cost you a lot and you and your crew might loose the motivation.

 You will be shooting approximately 80 pages in total for your first feature film. If you shoot three pages a day this will make your shooting period a month. Shooting three pages will be very easy, you don`t have to worry about extending your shooting schedule. In the first week you will realise your shooting speed and you will decide to shoot faster for your next movie. With your experience and your knowledge from the first movie, you will be able to write and produce your second movie accordingly.

4.3 Don`t Forget Anything Behind!

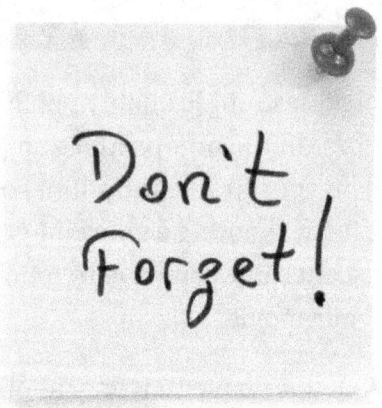

Ok I know you don`t have trucks full of  film equipments with you on the set! However what you have are important for you, your Dslr, your lenses, lights, butterflies, microphones, tripods etc. Maybe you`ve borrowed it some of them from your friend, or have rented them. So it is important to keep them together.

Between the scenes you might most probably change places and during this period lots of thing can be lost. You can assign a friend for the equipments, and give him a checklist for it, so that he can control whether each equipment is there or not.

 Preparing a check list is important, a little bit boring maybe but this will give you speed during the shooting period. Imagine that at the end of a shooting day, you and your crew are exhausted from working. You just want to shoot the last scene that`s planned, but bad news from your cameraman comes fast. "Bro, we forgot our light stands in the previous set". Great news, right. The set that you have shot your previous seen might be half an hour away. So, goodbye to the last scene!

 If you are prepared, you don`t need to face that kind of problems. By doing that you will seem pro and be a pro.

4.4 Rehearse More Than Anything

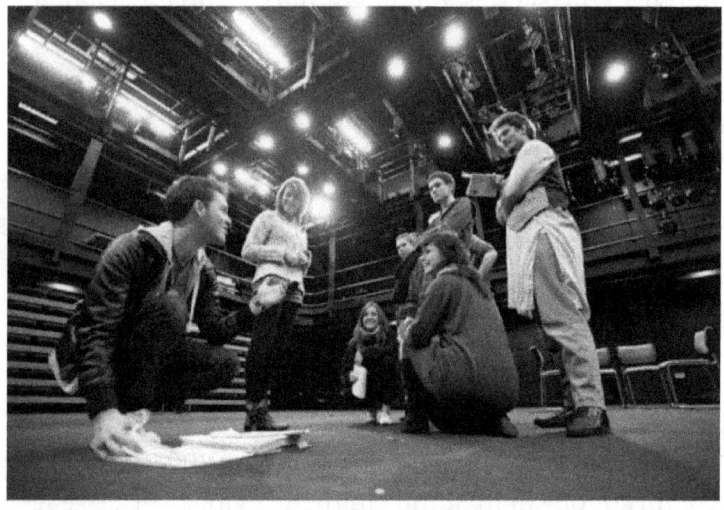

Most of you might think that rehearsing is before production, however even if you do so, if you have little time before the scenes, always make a fast rehearsal with your actors. By doing this, you will be sure everything is on track and this will give confidence to your crew and to your actors. You can even record the rehearsals which will make a great behind the scenes videos for you to use for the blu-ray of your movie.

Some directors prefer to do this on their sets, however it is costly, and in Hollywood set time is a great deal of money, and the producers do not usually let this happen. This is the fun part for us, you don`t have some greedy producers on top of your head so you are very much free to rehearse as many times you can. Remember, you are the producer of your movie.

 Don`t strech this too much because your unpaid actors/actresses and your crew might get tired of your perfectionist behaviour!

4.5 Cinematography Guy In The House

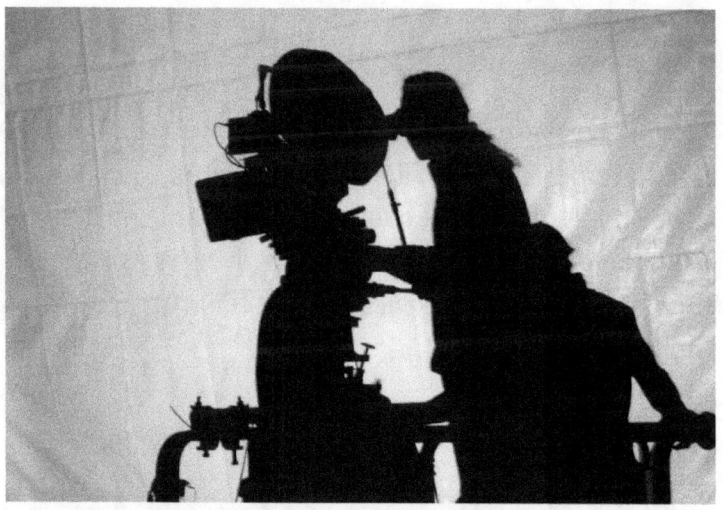

At the beginning of the book I have confessed you about my misunderstanding about filmmaking. I thought that it was all about cinematography, it was all about getting the best camera with the best lenses and use them to catch the best picture for the scene.

As we might all have realised, making a feature film is far from from those statements. However in the shooting process you can enjoy the freedom of getting the best shots for your movie.

For this please do not forget the basic three point lighting formula. It is better to lighten up your scene than getting it dark. By doing this you will have the chance to darken them in the post production process. Otherwise, with the dark scenes in hand you will not have the chance to lighten them up.

It will give a great production value if you use your DIY sliders, steadycam and all sort of stuff to make your shot look cool. Of course it will be appropriate to use them for the proper scene, however by using them you will get the sense to use them correctly for the right scene.

4.6 Sound Matters

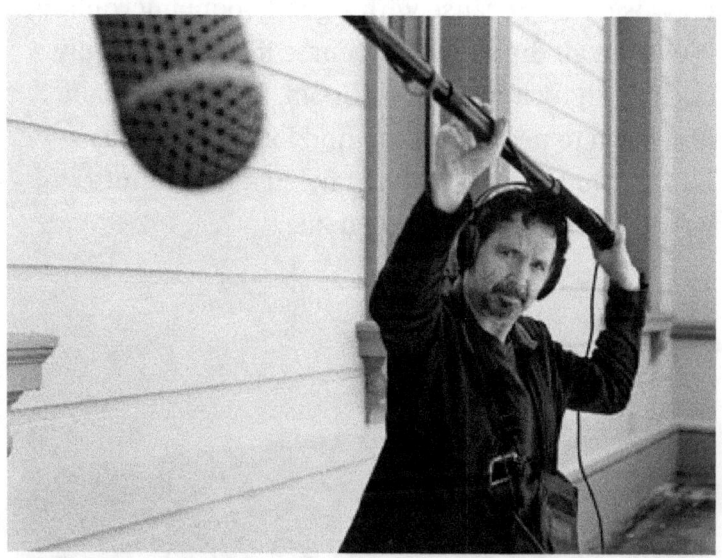

If you are going for a feature film, which you are, you need to have a good sound. So you can not even think about recording it directly to your Dslr or camera. As you might have noticed it before in your short films or in your videos, even they record stereo there will be lots of noise. Because they get the sound from everywhere, they can not able to directionalise it to the actor/actress. What you need is a boom microphone. You don`t have to buy a high price boom microphone. Rode NTG will be enough for your sound recording. Also please use it with zoom h4n or Tascam. This will make your sound almost perfect.

On the set, during the shooting be sure that all your crew is quiet. Because with a good boom microphone, it will get all the sound. Of course if your boom guy doesn`t know how to use a boom, be sure to make him learn to use it. You can find lots of great basic information about it. It will take just five minutes for you to learn how to use a boom.

4.7 You Need Storage Bro

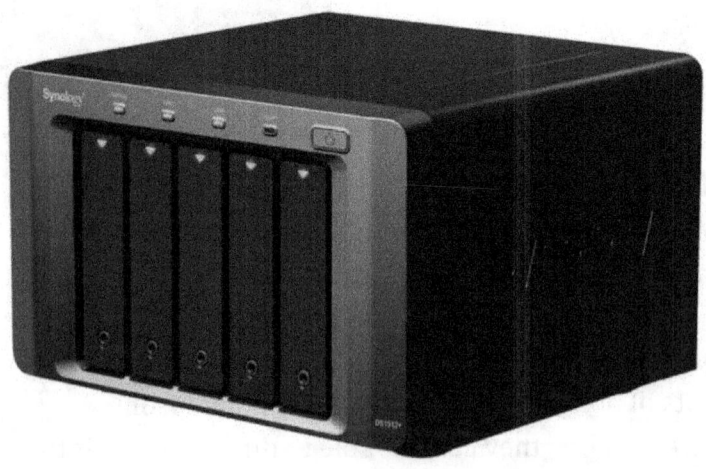

For a feature film you need a lot of storage for your videos. You will be shooting at least 1080p. Some of you have Blackmagic Camera or Canon C100 or C300, so you may go for a 2K movie. It might seem cool for some of you to shoot in raw, however when it comes to the post production process you will be f up! Why? Ever tried to edit 2K video in your home PC or Mac? The work flow will be devastating. And if you have never tried that before, do not be a hero before your first feature film. Save it for another time or be sure to handle the 2K raw video editing work flow before starting your shooting.

Even you shoot 1080p, you need a lot of sd cards and external drive for your movie. Probably 4TB of external storage will be enough. And for your Dslr you need to get at least 4 of 128gb of sd cards which you can shoot your film in it. Also it will be good to upgrade your PC or your Mac a little bit, because you will be working on big files while you are editing, and that means a lot of rams, and cpu power if you want to work fast.

4.8 I Need Food Man!

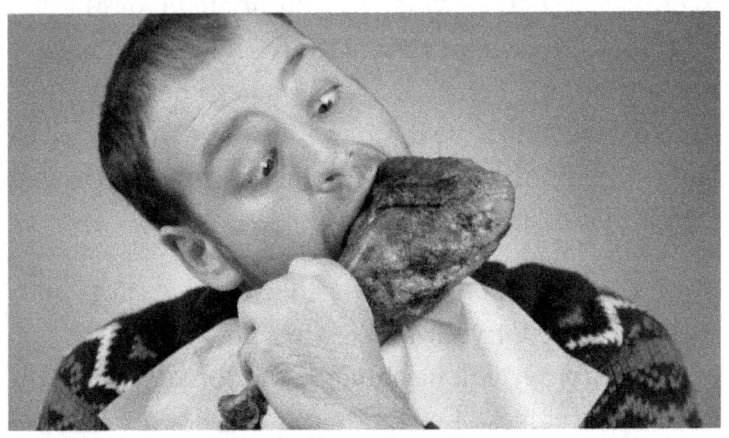

Who doesn`t, right? Remember you are making an independent film with almost no money, no sponsors. But if you think filmmaking as a career, you have to take good care of your technical crew and actors and actresses. So they will keep working with you, and your reputation as a filmmaker will go up by word of mouth.

Now let`s cut to the chase, if you don`t give them money, you should at least be sure that they eat great food. One way to achieve this is, to find your relative with the best cooking ability and ask for her/his help. Provide the supply to her/him and he/she will cook for your crew. Assign one person from your crew, mostly it will be your 14 year old cousin, to be the food distributing manager (yeah, you can even make this job title up, just for him).

Always obey your lunch and dinner times, as you have scheduled before, so that your crew will work without questioning about the meal time and concentrate on their works. This will create a happy environment for the crew, which will be nice for such stressful long shooting hours.

4.9 Wrap It Up, and Party!!!

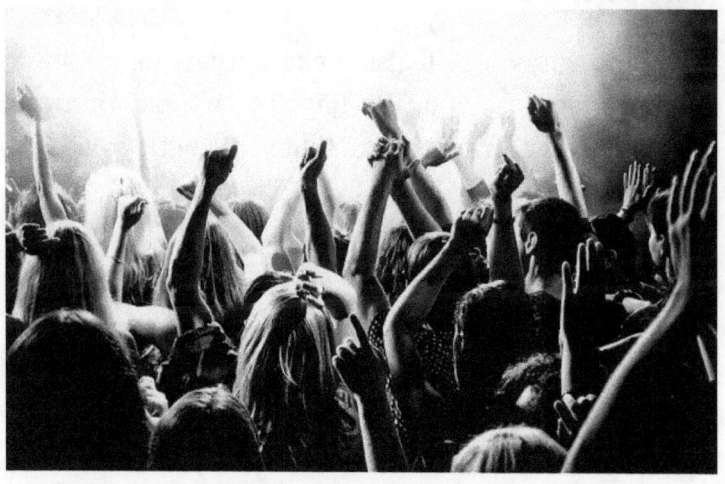

Can you even believe that this the last day of your shooting! Probably in your last day, you will be shooting your extra scenes, or the scenes that you missed to shoot in its own day. So, your set will be very light, a little bit tired, however happy because of completing something that they have started.

 You as a filmmaker, be the best of yourself in the last day of your shooting. Don`t be in a tired, I`m the director and I did this all by myself mood! This your last day to charm, and to appreciate all the people that have helped you to make this dream come true. So respect this, and prepare your finishing party! It doesn`t have to be a Jay-Z kind of party, a nice cake and good beverages will be enough. Maybe some baloons and some ornaments will make the mood more party like.

 By doing this, you will also make a great behind the scene material for your Blu-Ray. Oh, I almost forgot, don`t you ever forget to take that selfie with your crew!

5 Post Production

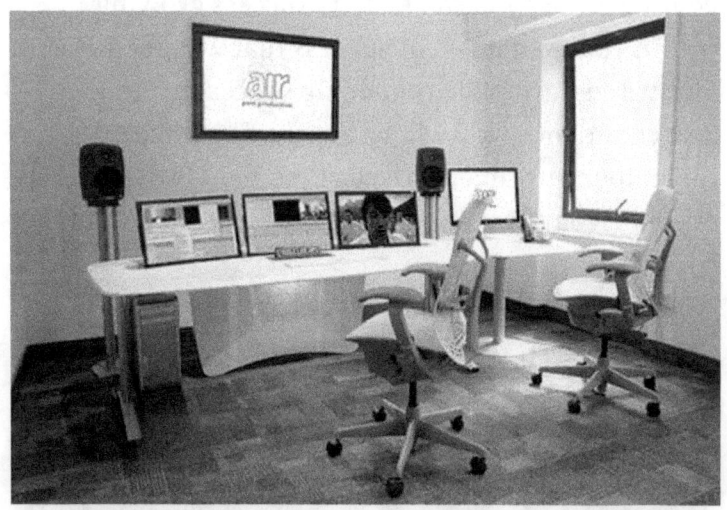

Before talking about post production stuff, just hold it! Do you realise you just finished shooting your first feature film! Can you believe this? Take a deep breath and think about what you are about to achieve!

You might have some doubts about your scenes that you have shot. You might have had some cinematography problems, sound problems, maybe some acting problems. Never mind those! I am not saying this because you can just handle them in the post production, I am saying this because whether you have shot a lot of scenes with some problems, you just made it. You now have something to work on, to edit in front of you now. And you are almost done.

Remember you are not finished yet, but as you close your eyes now you can feel the success growing within you. And it is that success that will keep you motivated during the remaining processes. And with that confidence, you will be a great filmmaker. Always remember this time, that exact moment is the process of you becoming a real filmmaker. Now, let`s go on!

5.1 Just Watch What You`ve Got!

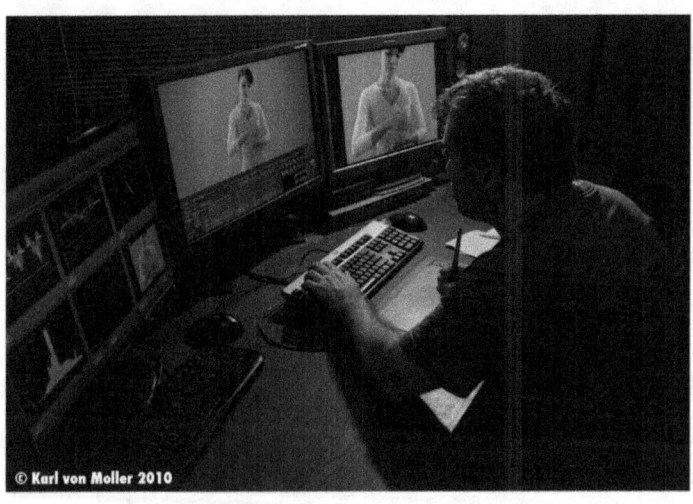

© Karl von Moller 2010

I hope you have given yourself enough time to rest a little, because post production is the part most of the new filmmakers underestimate! This won`t be like shooting a short or a Youtube video and edit it with a cool music that you have picked! That`s right, it will take almost 2 times the time in regards for production. You heard me right! And I assume that you don`t use too much off CGI for your first feature, if you did, it might take more than that.

Ok back to the subject now after giving that short notice! For some of you this process of watching all your scenes might seem boring. However if you are this kind of person, you might as well have not labeled all your scenes after the shooting! If you did, good for you. However most of the time, because the shooting period is such a mind blowing and time consuming process, directors don`t have the time to watch the scenes that they shot during the day and label them. So pick your wing man, let's call him your editor, and watch all the shots and label them. By doing this you will make the editing process easier for your editor or for yourself. (I consider that you might be the editor)

5.2 Back Up, Back the f#&%k up

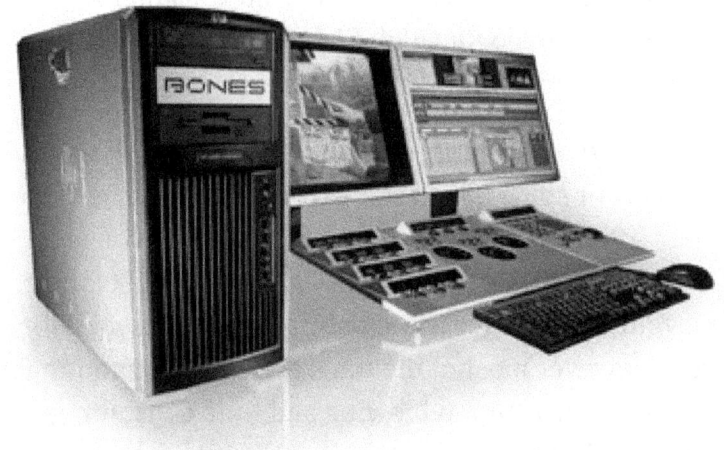

I know that this part`s title is a little bit harsh, but this is deadly important for your editing process. As short filmmakers we have the instinct to shoot and edit and upload it on Youtube workflow. In this workflow, we don`t need to back up our shots because we have so little and the work for it is not so complicated. However in a feature film you probably have at least 50 short videos if I may say! Furthermore, in that size of video you can easily loose them during the editing process.

 So, please borrow some external discs and back up all your footage. It will be great if you have the storage to back them twice. So you will not have to worry to lose all or some of your work which you will be very sorry for.

And, why give someone to find your lost footage, and be another Paranormal Phenomenon through your work!

5.3 Using The Right Editing Software

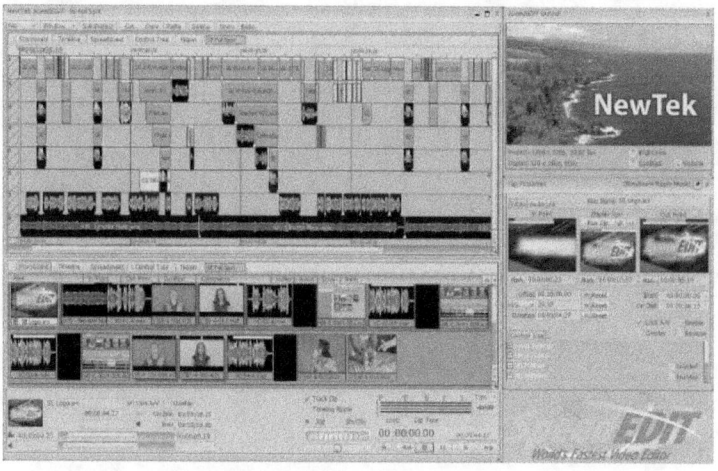

Well, we are not going to use windows movie Maker as we all assume! Some of you use Adobe Premier, some of you use Avid Pinnacle Studio, for some of you it is a different story. Whichever editing software you use for your editing process be sure that it can handle more than one working channel for video and sound.

This is important because you are going to work with more than one! The two softwares which I mentioned above are both capable of doing that. However if you are using another software and do not have time to learn a new one, be sure that it has those features.

Also, try to learn all the different features of your editing software which will directly influence your films success. Some of them have already built-in applications that you can use for small effects. There are also lots of external plug-ins which will make your job easier.

5.4 Color Correction is The Key

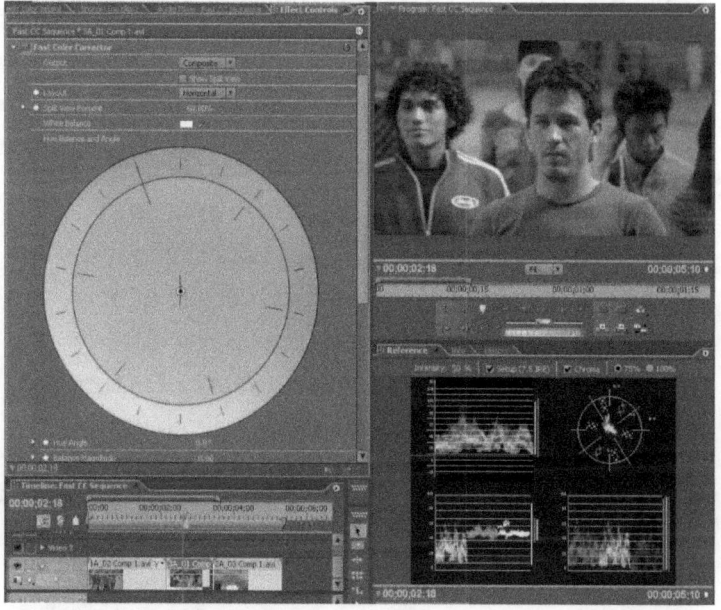

I always wonder how they achieve that incredible
look in Hollywood movies! In my short films and you
tube videos I tried to do that, of course it was just a
bad copy of a good masterpiece. I know that there are
hundreds of videos about how to achieve the
cinematic look with your dslr cameras. They are all
OK, however that kind of looks' secret is the
combination of different factors. First, you need a full
frame dslr camera, which is mostly known as Canon
5d MK2, Canon 5dMK3. So if you can find those
cameras that will be a great start for your film look.

Than as we all know, the lens factor comes to the scene. It will not be easy with your kit lenses to get the cinematic look! Lenses are the most important factor for your cinematography which defines the Hollywood look. It will bring a huge production value if you can rent or borrow some 1.2 stop lenses. You will get your bokeh, which creates an amazing cinematic look. With those lenses your night shots will also be great, because those lenses get the light in, and your scene will be brighter and less noisy. After you get the right cinematography in the shot, it is time for you to take it to the next level with your color correction software. There are lots of them on the Internet, just pick one and play with your scenes' tones till you find the right feeling for your movie.

5.5 Make Some Noise!

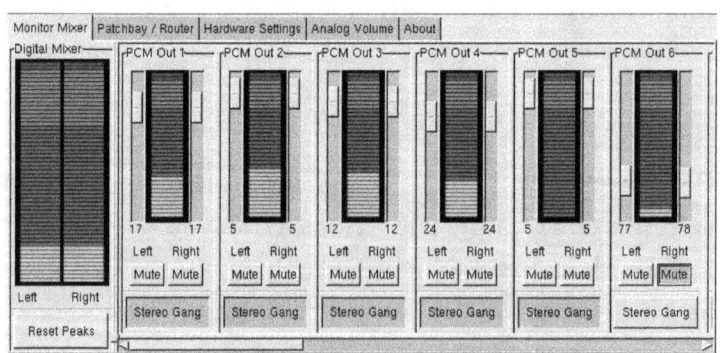

Not so much of course. I just want to be cynical for the sound design part. If you have implemented the things that I have told you before in the production process, you will probably have a good sound recording . However when you listen to it carefully you might find some problems, especially if you are listening to it from a sound monitor, you can catch every bit of a scratch in your sound. By the way, sound monitors are some great speakers which professional sound designers use while they are editing. They are a little bit expensive, however if you are on the way of being a filmmaker and if you choose to devote yourself to that job, those speakers will be a great investment for your business. If you can not buy or find one from a friend do not worry, your speakers will be OK for your first feature film.

I will give you a specific software name for you to make your sound quality perfect, it worked really fine for my projects. It`s name is Goldwave. A great software that you can get the most of your sound with it. Most of the professional sound designers use this software too. Give your sound a great importance, as it will make your movie more professional.

5.6 It`s Music Time Baby!

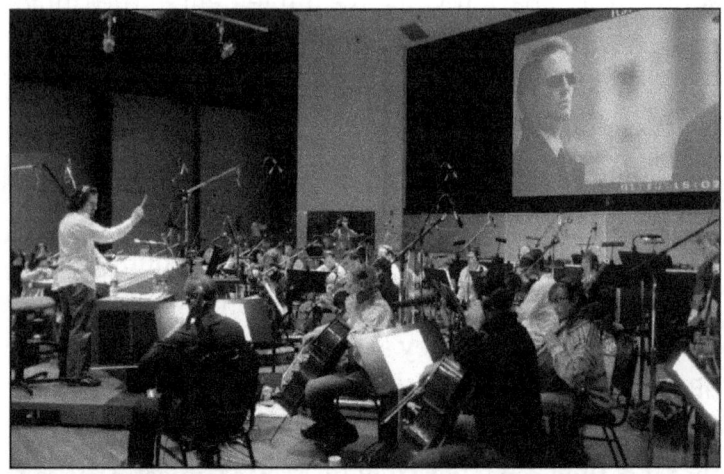

You might not realise how important the score of a movie till you have to edit your movie with great music! This will not be like finding the right song to a short video. You need some specific music tones for specific scenes, and they will all last for 5 to 30 seconds! Of course for some scenes it may be longer, however for most of your movie you need some short music.

 If you have a friend who can perform music and is willing to participate in your movie`s score, that will be great for you. If you don`t, don`t worry! There are some great music web sites that you can find your movie`s music. It will be a hell lot of a challenge for you, because you have to listen thousands of music to choose the right ones and use it in the movie. You have to be very selective, because otherwise you have to spend lots of money for them. Even though, music on those Internet pages are not very expensive, if you choose lots of it you will be spending a lot of money on them.

Remember, if you are thinking of participating in a film festival, you have to get the rights of the music that you are using for your movie.

5.7 Opening and End Credits

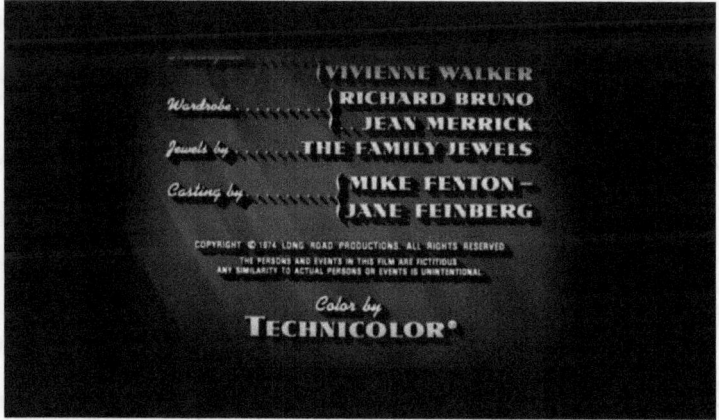

This seems like an useless subject for some of you but opening and end credits are like the cover of a book. It will be your movie's signature.

In the opening credits, you will give the audience the general feeling of your movie. In this part some of you might like to go with an animation or some detail shots about your movie. It depends on your movies genre of course. Furthermore you have to be creative here as this might be your signature as a filmmaker. Being creative does not necessarily means to make it complicated, it may be very simple. As I said before, it depends on your point of view.

For the end credits part, generally what they do is just to go with a black background and crawl the credits upward. If your movie is a comedy, you can use your funniest behind the scenes moments here.

5.8 Just Shorten It a Little

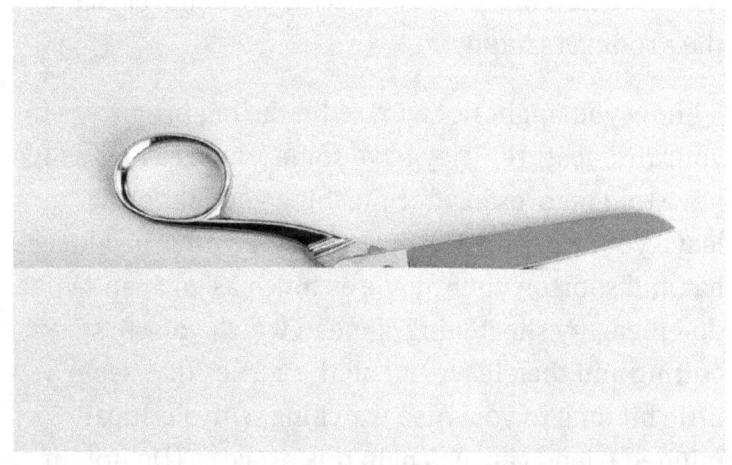

Do you know that almost all of the directors in Hollywood do not have the right to edit? Yeah, it might sound crazy, however this is the cold truth about them. If you are one of the directors of a blockbuster movie which is produced by a big Hollywood studio they do not let you enter into the editing room!

Enough about those very little known truths. I am going to tell you why the big guys do not let the directors in-to the editing. This is because if you are a director, it will be hard for you to get rid of the stuff that you have passionately shot. So you might want to use all your footage in hand which subjectively can make your movie a little bit longer than you have planned. This will let you to a boring movie which will make it a flop for the box office that will never make the producers happy.

 I know you might not work with the big producers in your first feature. They have some good reasons as I have told before. So after finishing your shooting, leave your director hat there and grab your producer hat and shorten your movie as much as you can. What do I mean by shortening? I mean watch your first editing and then leave out all the scenes that seem a little bit long to you. Also watching with a critical minded friend can also help this process. (Do not hit him very hard when he criticizes the scenes:)

5.9 The Last Cut

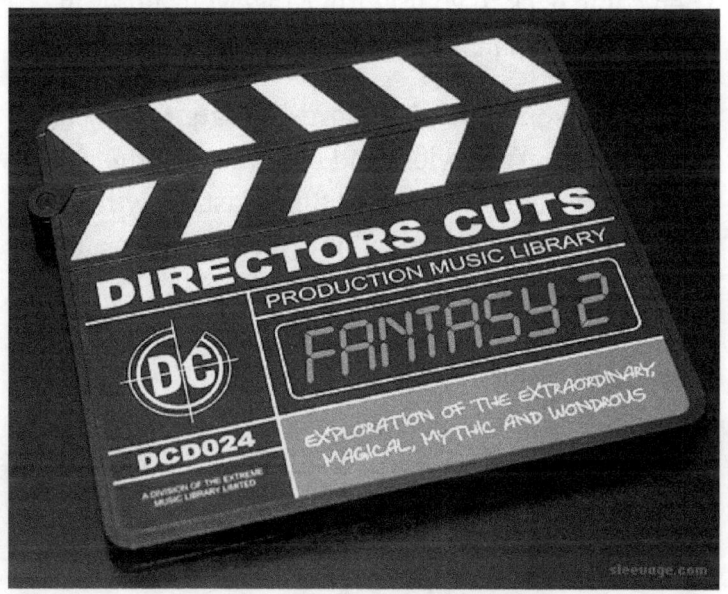

For the last cut of your movie, it is important that you had enough time to rest yourself and your movie. It is like the writing process, you have to get away a little bit from your project to evaluate it objectively.

What I mean by that is, in all of those processes, pre production, production and post production you get tired from your movie. I know it might be hard to confess for some of us however, it is almost always like that. So give yourself a break, but not too much! Just enjoy your success a little, you have already achieved a lot. This is almost the last process.

It depends on you, however 1week is enough to rest. Then come back to your editing, take your notes in front of you and make your last cut.

Make your sound balance more accurate, your scenes transitions more flawless and check every other detail. At the end, watch your film`s last cut with a critic alike friend. Listen to his or her opinions and finish it perfectly.

6 Marketing is Always Good

- Teaser
- First Look
- Theatrical Trailer Release
- Music Launch
- City Tours Begin
- Producer/Director's Interview
- Movie Premiere
- Movie Release
- Post-Release Follow-up

I want you to stop reading now, and just close your eyes. Think of what you have done;what you have achieved! You have finished your first feature film. I assume it has been a great journey for you and all the people who have worked with you during this period. This is a big achievement, however in order to win the big prize you have to make people know about your movie. And of course marketing is the way to do it.

When we hear the term "Marketing" we indy filmmakers get a little cold, but do not be! It is not always about huge amount of marketing budget and a creative advertising agency! What you can do is to replicate what they do in small terms.

What is your biggest weapon? You have the time to market your movie and the passion to do it well. As you are reading this book you have already learned a lot about filmmaking. And as you continue to read it, you are going to meet my old profession. A "Marketing strategist"! Yes, I wasn't born as a filmmaker, before finding my real passion in life, I was a marketing strategist for which I hold a college degree! It seems like I am bragging about it, however I just want you to know that I know about marketing a lot, and why not use it for filmmaking! Let`s do it, step by step!

6.1 When to Start?

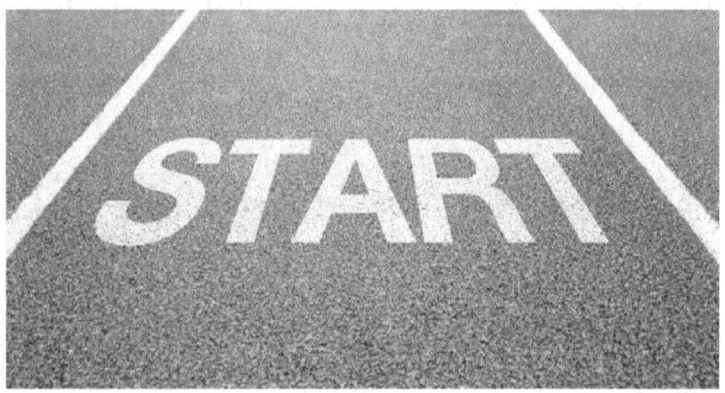

It is always better to start your marketing as soon as possible. We tend to market our work after it finishes, however if you named your project it is time to start marketing. Even before naming your project you can share your film idea with your social media friends. This will create the hype for your project. Everyone will ask you about it and wonder about your project.

You don`t have to name your project at the beginning just to market it. Mostly in Hollywood and in the feature film market they start their project with a code name. This is to protect the project from stealing.

However you don`t need to worry about others to steal your film idea. Because all you need to do is to make your first feature film to get your name out there.

So, as soon as you make up your mind about your project, market it in every social media platform, and in any other place that you can.

6.2 Where to Start?

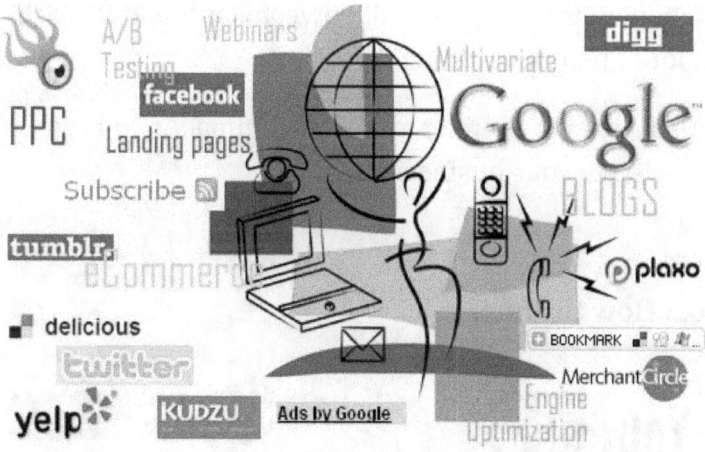

Of course you are not going to start from a newspaper by giving your advert. This will cost you a lot. As you can all predict we will start from our social media accounts. Facebook, Twitter, Google plus are so powerful that many big production companies are also using those platforms for marketing in addition to their other marketing platforms.

There are also lots of other new social media platforms that you can promote your movie. You can also write about your movie on your blog. Moreover you can create extra blogs to get attention and top your Google ranking as an indy filmmaker.

 If you have some money you can also spend it for social media advertising and some old school flyers about your movie. Do not underestimate the old school marketing, it is still powerful as you can reach a lot of people by doing it.

Also a small reminder, as a new filmmaker you can now have your business card!

6.3 How to Start?

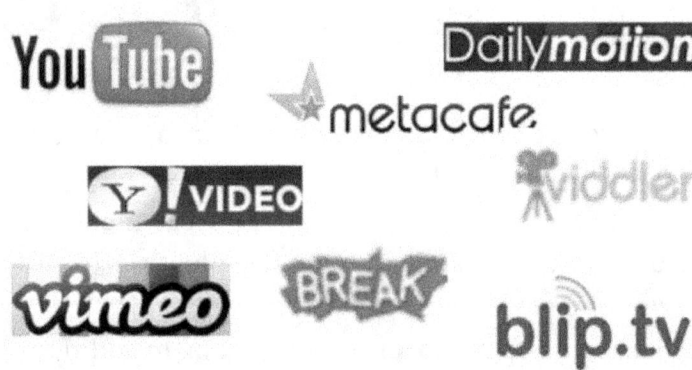

In the previous chapters I have already mentioned about them a little. The purpose of marketing your first feature film is, to become known as a filmmaker and to spread the word about your creativity with your movie. So if you are going to choose filmmaking as a career always be honest about your movie. However they say that marketing is always about exeggareting. They are mostly right. What you are going to market is your utopia, it is what you want to achieve. Do not forget about that!

You can start by preparing your teaser and promote it on youtube. Answer all the questions which come from your social media accounts. Prepare a great poster which is not going to be hard with today's technology. You can always find some free photoshop templates and change them a little which will make your movie`s appearance more professional.

In addition, you can prepare your movie`s web page on which you can give some free posters of your movie to people  signing to your newsletter. As doing so you can keep them informed about your movie`s updates.

6.4 How Much Do You Need?

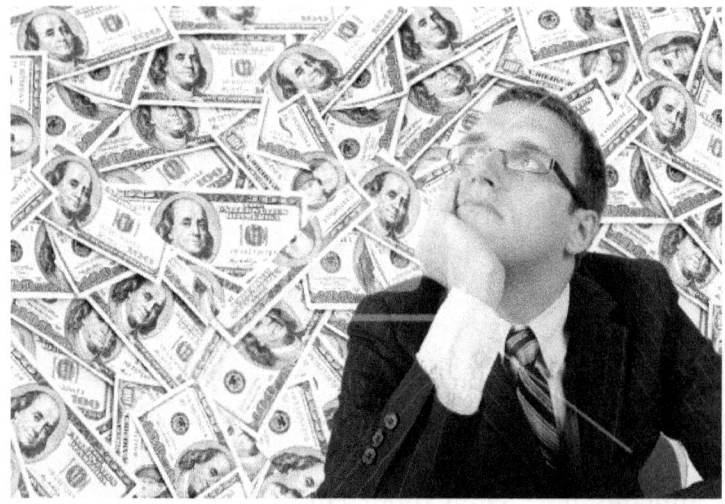

Not very much. You may be surprised by that answer however it is true for your first feature. You may not be able to get a distribution deal with your first feature. If you get that deal, good for you. The distribution company or the production studio will make the marketing for you. However this might be a little too optimistic.

Sadly we have to return to our reality and how we can make the most of it with our small budget. You have got to know that the more you invest in your movie the more you will get the word out there about it. So be sure that you invest almost half of your production budget for marketing your movie. Believe me, it will be appreciated by the time they see what you are doing with your budget.

Even after sending your movie to a festival, you can still continue to promote your movie.

6.5 Word of Mouth Of course!

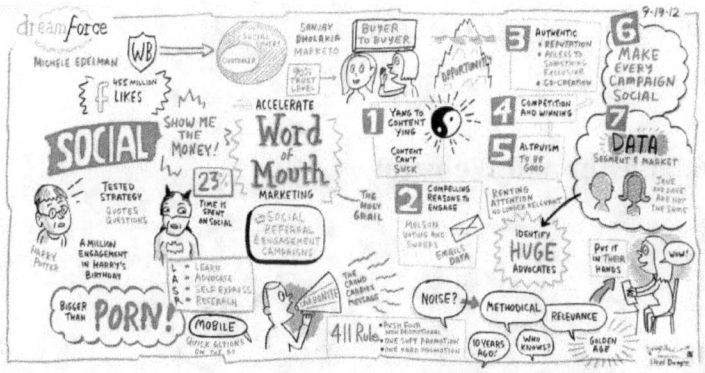

The best marketing method is not just paying to a creative agency and make a lot of promotions for your movie. It is word of mouth! The best way to promote your movie is to make it loved by the people who have watched it and spread the rumour that it is the best movie they have ever watched.

How can you achieve this? Simple! Just make a test screening for your movie to your best friends and relatives. And wait for them to spread the rumour and make your movie`s promotions for you. It will spread in a second. You can also make a screening in your school if you are a student. This will be also very cool for you I guess.

You might not be sure if they will say good things about your movie. Do not worry about that, even if you have made the best movie of the century, there will always be some idiots who will criticize it whether they like it or not.

6.6 Poster and Website!

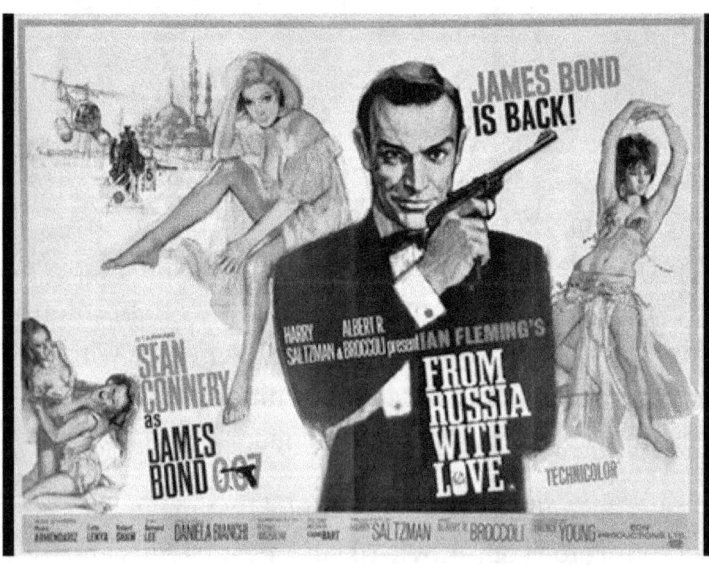

Here comes the cool stuff. It is time to "go Hollywood" as the good director Ryan Connolly says. It means that you will prepare your poster and web site as Hollywood movies do. How? Not too hard.

If you are good at photoshop software you are halfway there. You do not even have to design the whole process by yourself. There are lots of free poster templates out there. Also if you pay a little extra money there are services which can design it for you for a small amount of money. Just send them the pictures about your movie and some basic information about your subject, and they will do the job perfectly for you.

If you don`t want to pay any money or you don`t know how to use photoshop, you can always find a friend who might be interested in designing a poster for a feature film. For your website you can easily use the web site wix.com, for which you do not pay any money and you can choose from their big template library. There will be some adds appearing on your web site however if you pay 9 dollars/ month they will remove them. You can choose the monthly payment method because your film will be out there just for a short time. So you do not have to pay a yearly fee!

6.7 Do I Need a Red Carpet?

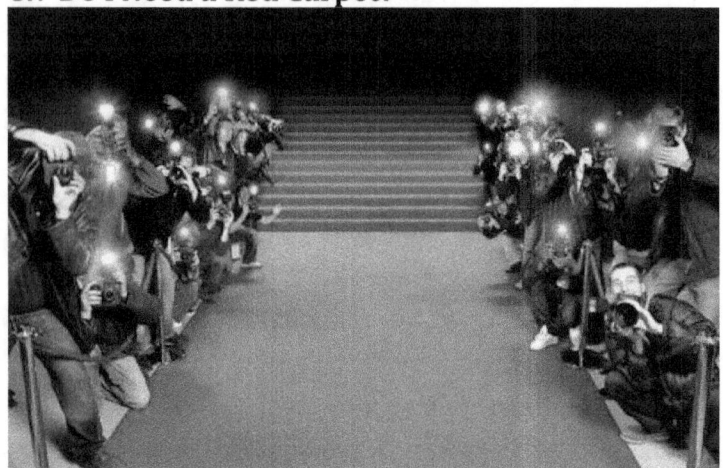

Why not? I think we all fantasies about walking down the red carpet. Maybe with our family, boyfriend or girlfriend.

If you don't like that kind of fancy shit, you are probably lying to yourself. We all secretly do want that red carpet! It is all about achieving something big. It makes you feel the glory of the job that you have achieved.

6.8 Don't Forget Old school!

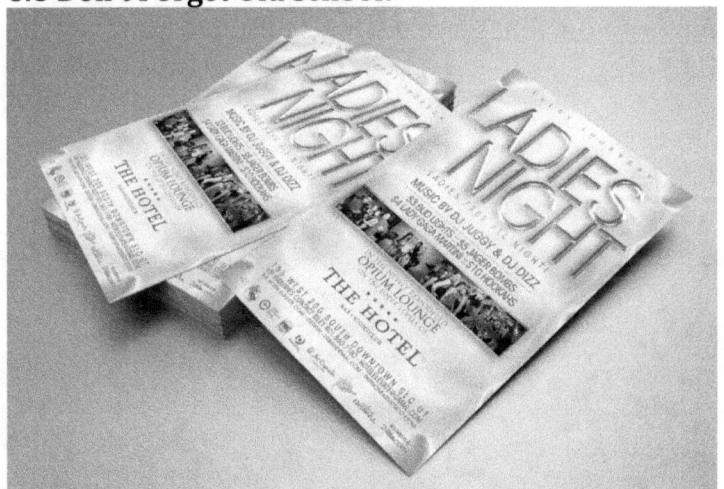

What do I mean by "Old School"? Long before the social media, there were flyers and those kinds of printed materials.
(I feel like a grandpa now) You might not think those methods are effective but there is a reason all the big companies still invest millions of dollars on those promotion methods. Because they are still effective.

You do not need to invest thousands of dollars on flyers, just get some copies and hand them out to your neighbors and relatives, so that they will know about you and your movie.
You can also talk with the local newspapers and magazines about your movie. They will be interested in your movie and you do not need to pay them any money. Most of them will be happy to help an independent filmmaker on the process. You can later

send them a copy of your dvd or the blu ray of your movie in the first place so they will know how special they are.

6.9 Keep It Clean

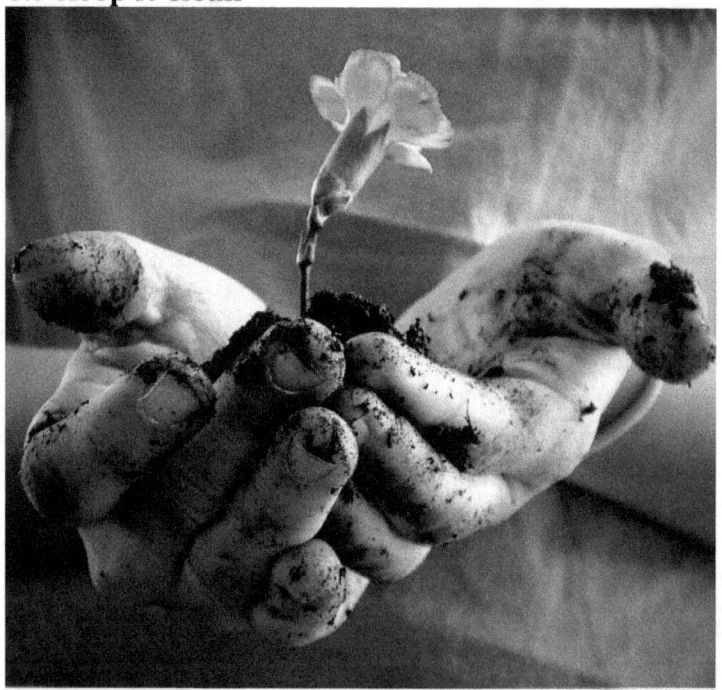

As you read the book you may have realised that I offer lots of different techniques in marketing. It is up to you to use all of them or just pick one and go with it. Always remember; simple is good. Always implement those promotion techniques in a simple way.

What do I mean by simple? Just make them clean, understandable, easy to grasp. Why do I say that? Because, sometimes when it is our first movie, we have the motivation to make the most clever marketing campaign in the world.

The disadvantage of this kind of thinking is, when you try to do something that hasn't been done before, you might "kitch" it. Kitch is an artistic word mostly used by artists for an art piece which is bad because it is over done. If you use too much detail in your art work, it mightget complicated and you might not give your message directly to your audience.
So, you can use this understanding for your movie and moreover for your movie's marketing.

7 The Final Round

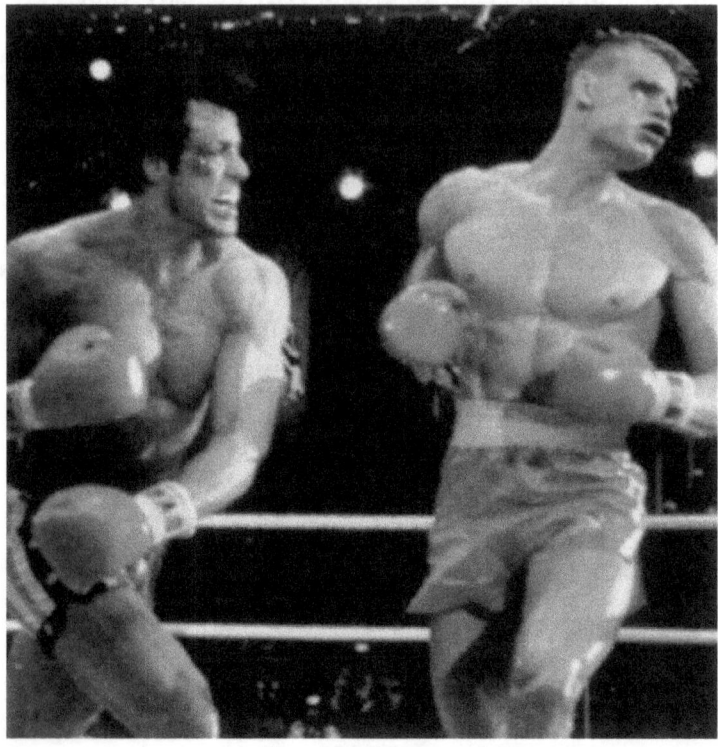

What is theFinal Round? It is where you take everything together and archive them. This process helps you to apply to film festivals in a more relaxed and prepared way.

 Do not be afraid of entering film festivals. I am saying this because when you make your first movie, it is possible for you not to like it so much and not to send it to a film festival.

7.1 Preparing the Teaser

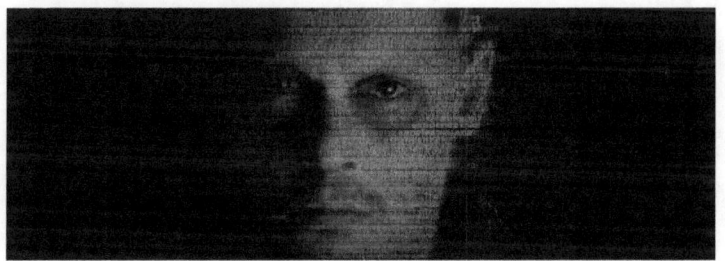

Whether you enter a film festival or share your film on an Internet video channel, it is important to prepare a superb teaser.

 The secret of preparing a killer teaser is to watch lots of teasers. Actually it is almost a science to prepare a good teaser. There are companies in Hollywood who are professionalized just to make teasers.

 It is all about mathematics actually. Don`t worry, you don`t have to be a mathematician to prepare your teaser. Just watch the teasers that are related to your genre and copy almost everything from there. I say "copy", because before you get the idea of making a good teaser, you can just copy the best and grasp the idea of creating a good one by yourself .

7.2 Gathering All the Documents

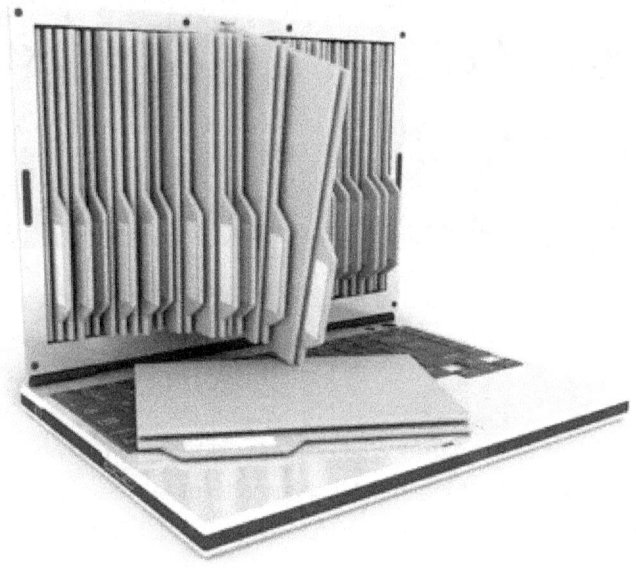

After finishingyour feature film it will be like going out of a big battle. You will be exhausted, however you will feel great for winning the battle. In this part I am going to remind you an important thing that most of the first time filmmakers mostly forget!

 Before entering festivals, making the blu ray of your film or uploading your movie on the Internet you have to gather all your documents together. What do I mean by documents? All your scenes that you have uploaded to your computer. This is important because probably you will have a little space in your computer`s drive and you should eliminate all the unnecessary scenes. You should probably get some external drives to archive those files.

Other important documents are the synopsis, treatman and the screenplay of your movie. Some of the festivals also request "The director`s opinion" that you can add to your documents. Your notes during the pre production period are also very important. Those will be very precious within years later when you will get back to those and seize your development about cinema.

Behind the scenes part is important too. Also there will be a lot of unnecessary parts that you do not want to add to your blu ray disc. Also keep them in your external drive and you can watch them with your children, friends or family some years later just for fun.

You can add all the pictures that you have taken during the production process of your movie, which will help you when you are interviewed by a magazine or a newspaper.

7.3 Entering the Festivals is Great

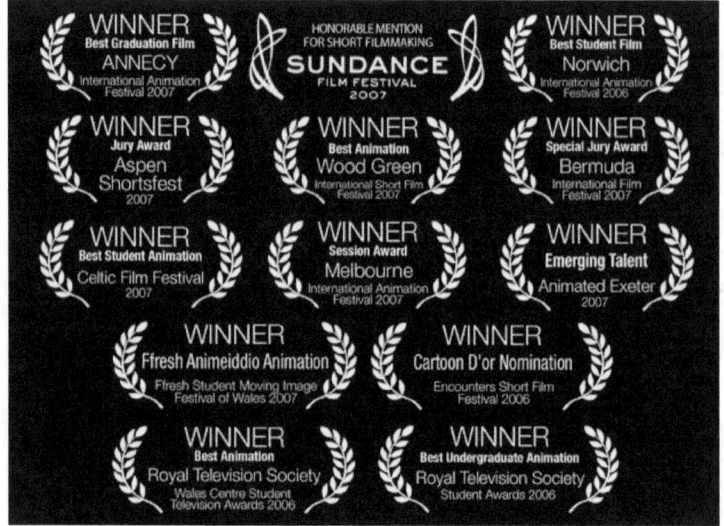

Now you have your film with you. You are ready to enter the real world of cinema. And the traditional way to do this is to enter the film festivals.

If you believe that you finished a masterpiece and you are the next Tarantino you can enter the best film festivals which will cost you a lot. Why? Because these festivals are old, they have been out there for years and every important producer, talent manager enters these festivals and find the next talented filmmakers. I know these are great news for you, however if you are entering these film festivals with your first feature film you might end up not being accepted to these festivals. I don`t want to be the guy who give bad news to you which would be the opposite side of this book, but there is a big chance they will not accept your movie and your money will go down the drain. If you really want to enter these festivals and get the attention of the movie world you might start from the new film festivals and be accepted or even win a prize from the jury. It will be easier and will encourage you to enter the film festivals that will take you to Oscars with your second or third movie.

Please don`t judge me for being realistic in this subject, but I just want you to be a filmmaker. Entering a big film festival and not even being accepted by them can break your enthusiasm which can lead you not to be a filmmaker and doubt about yourself.

Ok! We are done with the bad news stuff. Now it is time for the good news. There are lots of ways to enter the film festivals. You can browse all the good film festivals from one web page and enter them online.

I will give you two of them. They are the most known and very affective web sites which will reduce your job during the entering process.

The first and very well known one is "Without a box". The first short that I made was REQUIEM and I used Without a box to enter Cannes Film Festival and Chicago International Film Festival, and the process was really easier than the old school model. You can check it out.

The second web site is Filmfreeway. This site is hilarious and I am now using it for my feature films. It is newer than Without a box, however their service is cheaper and they are on a good path.

You can check those sites and find out which film festival is for you and enter them via those sites by uploading your movie.

7.4 Interviews with the Vampire

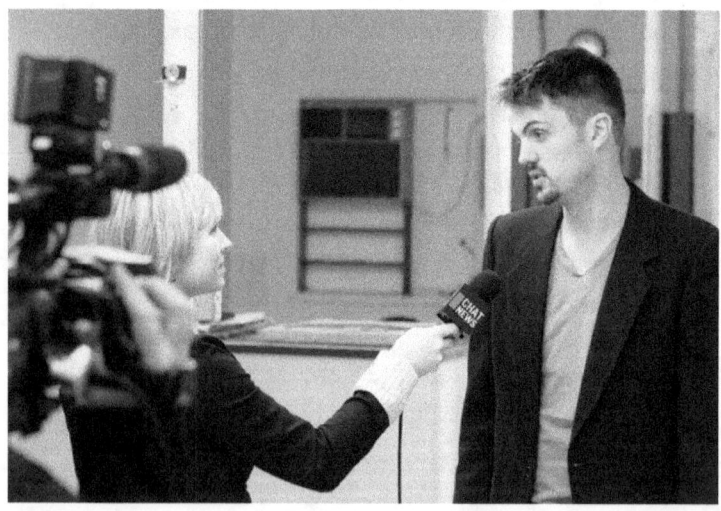

After you enter the film festivals and luckily got accepted, you will have the chance to win a good prize. By prize I mean you will get some attention from the movie community and the magazines will want to interview with you. There are also lots of well known bloggers who are watched by lots of film enthusiasts. So, you have got to be ready for these interviews.

They will ask you lots of questions about your movie, your characters, your view about life and every other detail. You can check some of the movie magazines interviews with the best known directors and have a hint about how they answer those questions.

7.5 Distribution is HARD or NOT?

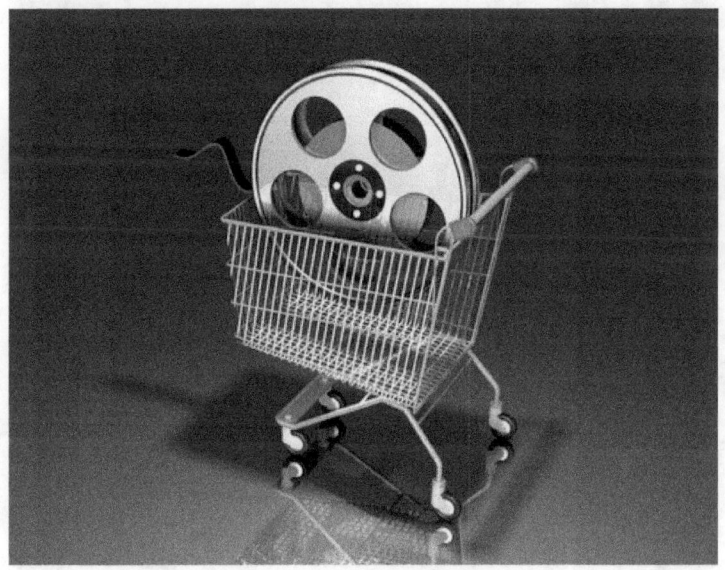

For your first movie you may have a little chance to get your film to a big distribution company. However if you are lucky and did a masterpiece as Tarantino your film might be realised by some distribution companies and producers or agents. In festivals it will be good for your reputation to meet with the agents and producers by person. If they know you by person they will realise how talented and passionate you are. This will give your film the chance to be distributed by the big distributors.

7.6 This is Your Business Card Baby!

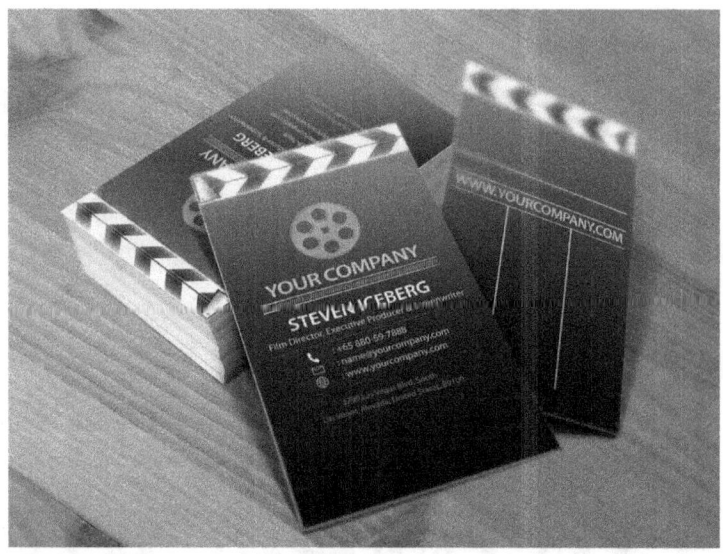

You might not find this very effective as an Internet era person however believe me it still works. It will be great for you to design and print a great business card for your career.

First of all, you can hand it over very quickly. It still gives a good impression to people when you hand over your business card. It shows that you are serious about what you are doing. Furthermore, you can use it in every film festival you go to in order to promote yourself and your movie. You will be memorable if you design a good business card. At the back of the card you can even put your movie's poster or a design that represents your movie so that the producers or talent agents can relate you to your movie.

7.7 Cinema Club

After you have finished your movie, and have made a little PR of yourself and the movie, you might not admit it but you are a kind of celebrity. Well, let's not call it celebrity, but you will be known by the cinema industry and the "geeks" who follow the industry. That means that you will have the oppurtunity to gather those people around you who are interested in making movies. You are an accomplished filmmaker afterall.

By doing that you will have access to a lot of talents, actor or crew wise. That will be your own "Cinema Club". You shouldn't skip that important mission of a cinema club, because that will not only help you to get the human resources that you need for your next movie but also they will create a legacy for you whether you want it or not.

So, be polite to your followers!

7.8 Making Your Own DVDs and Blu-Rays

Actually as you are reading my book you may have sensed that I am very optimistic or we can call it passionate about Filmmaking. You might have got the feeling that everything about filmmaking is a piece of cake and you can finish it in one day and be a filmmaker. Sorry my dear readers, as you might have already noticed; life is not that easy. I am not saying that the previous parts of my book are all about optimistic ideas. They are all very real, they are all very simple but the thing is, it is hard sometimes to go and do something, to get into action. Actually this book is all about to make you do this. As a filmmaker myself, who had finished his first feature film, I promise you that if you start and follow the steps in my book you will have your first feature length movie.

I am writing these lines because, after you finish your movie, it might not be distributed, it might not be accepted by film festivals. So what will you do then? Stop and cry about it? No, never! This is the beginning of your movie career. Every succesful person in this life has started his/her career by failing. When you fail you will learn from your lesson and continue from where you are.

What you can do with your film is, to print it to DVDs and Blu-Rays if you can. Put it on Vimeo which has a new feature "Video on Demand", that people pay money to see your movie online. They can rent it or buy it. You can sell your DVDs and Blu-Rays on your movies web page. Or you can just give them for free to the people who are interested to see your work. You can start with your family members as always. But please, please never give up!

7.9 Say Goodbye to your Baby

I know it is hard for you to say goodbye to your first born baby, however you should leave it to start your next project. It will be hard, I know that, I have been there.

You do not have to forget about it, you should just empty your head to start the new one. You can still promote it from your social media pages or via your movie's web site.

But now it is time to move on!

-The End-